Capital of Spies

DG

Published by DG, 2024.

CAPITAL OF SPIES

First edition. April 7, 2024.

Copyright © 2024 DG.

ISBN: 979-8224714117

Written by DG.

Table of Contents

Book Title: Capital of Spies
Author: Daire A Guiney

Introduction

The objective of this book is to provide a comprehensive yet simple guide to general computers users of the dangers of internet products and services and the safe guards that you as a digital user in the twenty first century can employ to prevent such things as you online internet presence and profile from being compromised, the most common form of internet hacks, how they have evolved and grown and how the prevalence of digital devices in our lives can cause hidden dangers to our children, friends, families and work peers.

This unofficial guide to the internet of things will show common pit falls of internet shopping, how financial institutes try to safeguard our financial information from being compromised, what data breaches are and what they mean to us, and the hardware and software of the Internet used to stop financial scammers.

This book what put together as a response in seeing numerous people that I know being friends, families and relations being targets daily by internet scammers either getting hold of their personal mobile number and spamming them with text messages and emails pretending to be from their bank, government department or a delivery company trying to make a delivery and requiring more information.

As a result, I hope the information is this book will prevent these same internet scammers from obtaining their personal information.

They would regular ask me how do I get rid of the? The only thing I could say is change your number because once they have your mobile number you will just start to receive more and more text messages and there is no end in sight. When you do get a new mobile number do not give it out to anybody you do not trust. And this was the best advice I could give them at the time.

Now with a bit of research and more day-to-day experience in the types of threats facing the public, I have put together this book to help the non-technical but user of internet devices against fraud and misinformation.

So go head, read on, and enjoy at the same time as understanding how to best protect yourself against all the threats the internet can bring upon you but also the many benefits.

The most common used software, hardware and best practises to internet security will also be looked at.

As people's homes and lives get more complicated by the amount of technology growing around, this gives practical and sensible advice on how you can safeguard your digital profile as a boss, employee, parent, or citizen.

The target audience of this book is those persons who may have a few smart or internet enabled devices used every day in their lives but are aware of the ever-growing threat to their internet lives by unknow assailant in other parts of the world.

After reading this book you will know what is required for you not to be the next internet victim scammed of their bank details unwittingly while going about their daily internet tasks.

The cyber security book for doers not dummies is comprehensive yet concise enough for you to read and understand.

Chapter 1 – Types of Cyber-Attacks

Every day around the world users of the internet is bombarded with attempts to compromise their online profile and presence. Most of these attacks may be never seen by the average internet users as they are most likely stopped by user's Internet services provider, Internet subscription service provider or their email hosted provider, however these attacks occurs and people in far of countries are specifically employed to use any available avenues to gain access to an internet users bank or online profile details. However, some of these cyber-attacks do make it through various security mechanism designed specifically to stop such attacks from occurring.

Such Internet service provider, and content provider as Google, Microsoft or LinkedIn employ specific technical expertise to thwart these attacks. This may include blacklisting countries, domain, or individual users from accessing their internet services. For you as an average user, you will never see the level of complexity required to keep an internet service up and running but may only see a snapshot of the type of attacks that makes its way through the internet and to your screen.

An Internet service provider has been traditional the organisation responsibility to providing a data connection to the internet, original over copper telephone lines but predominantly over fibre optic cables laid in the ground.

An internet content provider is an organisation that has evolved as a provider of internet content and services. They are either free, subscriptions service or generate revenue from advertisement or a combination of all three.

Each attack different levels of complexity but the objective is always the same for the data harvester or financial scammer. That is they want your financial details so that they can extracted monies from your financial institutes' accounts.

CAPITAL OF SPIES

A Data harvester is the person who searches the internet and other information libraries about an individual or organisation, to build up a picture about a person to be used for nefarious reasons such as attempts to sell you non exiting products or services or compromise you bank accounts and other internet accounts. This information is normal sold on to person who directly act on the information. The cost to ascertain this information is based on information that has been verified and is complex in nature provides detailed information about an individual's personal information such as lifestyle, internet subscriptions and financial records.

A financial scammer is nothing new to society and they act on information provided by a data harvester.

Some of the names of these type of attacks employed by financial scammers range from spam mail which is an open ended invite to access an internet link to phishing attacks which requires a little bit more work on behalf of the data harvester as they may know a little bit about you already such as which bank you bank with or which utility companies you use and tailor a specific communication masquerading from that financial institute or utility company.

Smishing is where a data harvester has got hold of your personal mobile as they feel this is a more direct communication to you rather than an email and are sending communications pertaining to be from your bank or utility company. The reason why they use utilities companies is that most people have monthly direct debits or standing chargers as a or renter to utility companies or media and telecoms provider. As a result, these companies have a record of your financial details on their systems.

Many services provider such as utility companies are aware of this and do employ specific layered security approach to safeguard your financial details however this does not extend to masquerade attacks and their only approach in this instance is to communicate warnings to their customers.

These warnings take the approach of text messages and emails, the same channels of communication that a data harvester would use to ascertain personal details from you. Your only approach is to screen all communications from text messages or emails pertaining to be from a specific company.

To screen form of communication for authenticity there are a few approaches that you can take. This includes ensuring that the email is sent from the actual companies' internet domain and not through an email from a free email web service with aspects of the companies address in the email address. To check the ownership of an internet domain of an organisation you can run an internet service query using whois.com to see registered address and content persons.

Another approach is what is called social engineering in where a data harvester will pertain to be from a specific company and will try to trick you into giving your internet account details. This may take different forms such creating a fight or flight situation by putting you under pressure during a phone call to respond to a situation which they have created without question the validity of the situation in the first place. It is common for persons employing social engineering approaches to use phone calls or what apps message to manipulate you into given them access to your financial information. These new age con artists approaches have not changed however their method of deliver has evolved with the times.

The underlining security message is always verifying the authenticity of all forms of communication before responding or actioning. These simple steps could save you money, your reputation, your career or even your mental health as these types of scammers do not give up easily and once they have a byte and have opened a form of communication with a financial scammer, you have verified to them the existence of a person to a name, email account or even postal address. Do not give your personal information out freely to anybody unless there is a specific reason, need, or business case that has been verified before being actioned.

Methods to verify a form of communication include asking for any telephone caller for a phone number to respond to, postal address or managers name to respond to. If in any doubt hang up the phone call, deleted the email or text message or bin the letter before you side with the financial scammer.

Siding with the financial scammer means that you allow to justify the reason for receiving a specific form of communication without realising that the need did not exist in the first place, the service does not exist with the service provider in question, or the message seems too outlandish to be real.

For many years people are aware of scams by post such winning in the pools, sweepstakes or informed of a rich benefactor or receiving a large inheritance, however the theme of hope that resonant in many forms throughout our society has cause people to not err on the side of caution but instead to side with the financial scammer and feeding their addiction for hope and financial scammers attempts to have you believe something that is untrue, unwarranted or unrealistic.

As humans it is important to question all forms of communication, including the spoken word as to whether someone is expanding upon a lie for their own benefit, and we are the party they are trying to exploit.

Other forms of attacks included silent attacks which unbeknownst to us, persons may be compromising our devices and installing tracking software such as keyloggers. Keylogggers are pieces of software that are silently recording and inputs on our devices and then sends them back to a server, third party or company to ascertain login credentials for internet accounts.

Malware is another form of s and can been seen as a poison pill in that you have applications installed on your device that are not for their intent reason. They are most likely infected with computer virus. How they operate has evolved through the years and now these applications do not become infected until they have an internet connection. That is the application will install perfectly normally on your device and may be downloaded from legitimate sources such as Google or Microsoft app store but as soon as they have an internet connection, they will download hidden packages and payloads and install them in your operating systems folders for nefarious reasons. The application may operate perfectly normally on the surface, but they are masking their true intentions. Always have you anti s application signature file updated regularly which detects new and evolving internet viruses.

An evolving and increasing threat with increased availability of free publicly available WIFI is fake internet routers and Wi-Fi signal. These routers may be broadcasting an internet channel that is free to access for users, but your devices details, and meta data is being harvested for nefarious reasons. This information will be sold on to the dark web where data harvester will parse this information with other information and create data packs.

Data packs maturity level varies according to the amount of information on a specific user. The more information the more expensive to purchase this information. People who purchase this information then behave like cold callers who building up this information even further to a point that the information can be monetize and sold again or acted upon. By acting upon we mean that attempts to compromise your internet account will be realised and they may employ such techniques as social engineering, cold communications or tailored responses, The most dangerous form is the man in the middle attack, where just like it sounds, they will pertain to the acting on behalf of another organisation for either a survey, to verify users details and other nefarious reason.

Man in the middle attack also extend to network devices where a network router may pretend to be associated with a specific network, but it is masquerading as a device not connected to a specific Wi-Fi SSID, domain name or internet service provider.

Ransomware is a dangerous evolution of computer viruses on the internet. This is where your computer's hard drive becomes locked, and data encrypted by a third party. To unlock your computer, you are required to pay a ransom and in exchange receive a decryption key that will unlock your computer's hard drive. The ransoms are normally paid using a crypto currency such as bitcoin. The decryption key will unlock your computer making it usable again and return your computer to its previous state. Most ransomware software uses zero-day vulnerabilities and exploitations. Zero-day exploits are like controlled explosions or gates to the city as in they are intentional put in there by the operating system manufacturer to draw cybers hackers to research one aspect of an operating system which seems to contain vulnerabilities while not exploiting other aspects of the operating system which may have genuine security flaws yet to be patched. So, zero days are intentional manufacturing or coded in flaws intended to control cyber-attacks or give ICT Security experts room to breathe in the event of a serious and organised broad and mass cyber-attack.

It has since come to light that a lot of these so-called ransomware attacks are not exactly encrypting your computer's hard drive, just the system files that you are using to view your computers content. The reason for this is that many hard drives these days have a huge capacity to store information with standard hard drives coming in at 256gb and can go up to one terabyte for some customisable computers. As such single file content these days is substantial for video, audio, and text file. That is to encrypt the full contents of a person's computer hard drive could take many hours if not days to complete. This service would have to be installed and run on your computer actively for a substantial and continuous period without being detected by you or your operating system IT security systems. This in computer terms is a big ask and as such the plausibility of these attacks must be questioned in its entirety. Also to encrypt files you need an exclusivity to have full read and write functionality to that file without any other profile or system resource or service simultaneously accessing that file at the same time. Also, as ransomware attacks large data servers in data centres, this make anyone wonder where the virus is coming from in the first place.

Thus, the conclusion is ransomware is a bit of a red herring in such that what we are really seeing is a pop-up screen with a threat message. This is the same as going into a bank and up to the bank teller with a threating letter demanding money when all you have is a banana in your pocket pointed at the bank teller.

Zero days are security flaws yet to be detected by the manufacturer of an operating system and as such security holes exist within the operating system in which computer virus are designed to exploit. They occur during the new development or version of an operating system were a new function or feature has been added and such by its inclusion has created a security hole due to interoperability with other functions of the operating system. This has not been discovered during the alpha or beta testing phases and when release to the public as a new operating system, normally as an upgrade to the existing operating system, this zero day will continue to exist until being exploited by a cyber-attack or been discovered by the operating system manufacturer and a patch or security update released to cover this security loophole.

Chapter 2 – Securing yourself against Cyber-Attacks

When using any technology either are own or work related, we must ensure that any information that we use these devices to create and transmit must do so in a safe a secure manner. As we have already highlighted there are many ways a data harvester or financial scammer to either compromise devices that you use or internet services that you use with the express intent on using this information for a host of nefarious reasons.

Key logging software can be installed on our devices. The best way to prevent this from happing is to always install operating system patches and updates which address security concerns or gaps with an operating system security architecture. Also installing the most recent update to an application from the web store where the application was purchased also address security concerns with applications that you are using on your device.

Avoid unnecessary free applications. The internet is synonymous with free internet applications and most internet startup will have offered a free version of a service or product to get market traction on the outlay, however this business model has been open to abuse where downloading an application may come with hidden applications.

This approach is called bloatware where other applications are bundled in with a download and installed on our device which may compromise the security of our device by overlaying existing system services or applications such as and intrusion detections systems. IDS are exactly what they sound like they detect any unauthorized access to out devices system folders or data folder. They are another layer in the security on the internet and are important in how they keep or data connections safe and secure.

Wireless devices. The introduction of the wireless protocol for data connection 802.11 a/b/c/g has allow users to become undocked from their desks and encourage users to move around their office building more freely. This technology has become ubiquitous and now wireless internet connection are available everywhere. This has come with additional and new dangers to the internet.

It is important to verify the network architecture that you are using be it at home or travelling. Avoid using free internet services and ensure that you have an adequate data plan with your mobile service provider. Using Internet sharing or hotspots from your mobile phones data plan for your laptop or tablet comes with some security concerns. Where internet sharing from your mobile phone, do not share the SSID of the network connection and associated passkey with anybody. Never use the same SSID and pass key twice. Always have your mobile device close to you and never leave your mobile down on the table beside you in thinking that you will get a better WIFI connection.

Working in public places should be avoided and working in shared offices or work hubs also comes with security concern. If using a pay as you go work hub, verify the legitimacy of the business that you are using as such services have been known to be set up for nefarious reasons. Again, the reason is for data harvesting. If a workspace seems cheap, running at a loss or something does not seem right then err on the side of caution and avoid. Some may be set up to attract professional persons and their internet traffic is monitored or 'managed' on their behalf.

Avoid opening your laptop or tablet in public places as this will always attract unwanted attention. The boot up sequence for all laptops and tablets for work purposes requires some form of authentication at start up. People will position themselves behind or beside you to garner security information and login credentials. This is the same with mobile phones were a user uses a screen lock pin. Again, these persons are data harvesters and will use this information in some form.

Malware is software freely available on the internet that can be downloaded for a specific function but contains hidden payloads, running windows services or other threats attached to these applications. As a result, any applications should be reviewed before being downloaded. Look at who the developer is, what platform you are downloading the application from, have you used any other application from this developer and if your own workplace uses this application for its specific function.

All applications on hosted sites such as Apple apps store or Google are vetted before being allowed to be published and downloaded from these application marketplaces. However, updates to these applications may cause them to become rogue and compromised by other third parties. This is no different to a computer viruses or bugs on an application yet to be coded out of them. When updating an application ensure that the update is coming from the platform from where you downloaded and install the application and not from any other site.

These sites may try to auto detect the applications that you have installed on your device and recommend updates or patches to s. What they are doing is not updating the application but installing bolt or add On's containing nefarious code that will take over the application and may allow your device to join a botnet. Your device once joined a botnet will run in a silent mode without you knowing about additional traffic being created by your device. This may turn your device into a mail server, pier to pier host or a member node of the dark web. This illegal activity may come to the attention of authority's who monitor international internet traffic. They will then be able to trace back the internet traffic to a specific internet node, router, and device.

The vast majority of ransomware comes across the internet either though a computer port or communication payload.

To avoid your computer becoming susceptible to ransomware firstly, always apply security updates and patches immediately to the operating system and restart your computer to allow configuration to occur.

Secondly, always access the internet behind a firewall, be it a personal firewall on your computer or on you network router.

Thirdly, never open emails with suspicious attachments.

Fourthly, use different technologies and operating systems if available to you. That is make use of the stable and security operating system of windows, apple OS, apple iOS and Google Android. Separate and segregate data functionality, application logic and operating systems were possible.

If using ad blocking applications either in a web browser or as an add-in, beware that this may prevent you from viewing certain internet content. Cookies are a mechanism that have been overused by internet companies in recent years. This functionality should have migrated to the web but has not. The reason for this as this gives web sites owners greater control over the content, they can display to persons who land on their web site.

Also, it allows web site owner to employ search engine optimisation algorithms to boost their Google search ranking. This is not to the benefit of customers or internet users at large. E you land on a new web page the website will ask you which cookies you want to enable. This is embarrassing for people of the internet age. Why we are still asked for this is a slowness of the development of web site creators to embrace new ways and technologies of internet functionality.

A website should be dynamic in nature and static by default. The full functionality of a website and associated content should be displayed always and if content deemed harmful or inappropriate by user's firewall, then this content should not be display. Everything else should be displayed.

It is good practise to use a web browser that can display all internet content in a safe and secure manner. The main web browser of the internet, Microsoft Edge and Google Chrome have been developed form the environment that they were native to as Microsoft Edge looks, acts, and integrates like a Microsoft product and Google Chrome looks, acts, and integrates like a Google product.

If you are used to applications from both internet service providers, then you should not have any issues working with both.

Also remember to disable auto fill and password manager for these browsers as data is stored in the browser and not in a separate and secure database. If you are fed up remember or creating password and think biometric login will solve everything to do with user authentication, then purchase a subscription to a password manager application.

This acts like an encrypted cloud hosted vault for all your password. When you reach a login screen for an application, your cloud login credentials will be automatically populated in the user login fields. You will still be responsible for the Multi Factor Authentication part of the login process.

Self-service password reset mechanism for your online account. Beware of employing this mechanism for your online accounts. If you forget your password, the best form of password recovery is using your username and reset code sent to your mobile device to reset your user account. Reset links to email account can be used by financial scammers for their own benefit by resetting your login credentials to login information that they have entered themselves.

If this service exists for any internet account that you have, disable it, and use the password reset function by reset code sent to your device. Also do not use the feature to create a list of backup recovery codes for your account as this is the same as righting down your password. If a cyber hacker gets access to these recovery codes, it will allow them to reset your account detail's without knowing you login credentials in the first place.

Fake online profile or sock puppet profile. It is increasing becoming the case that person's online identities are being clone and used in other parts of the world. This occurs were a data harvesters starts scrapping social media web sites, email threads and published information and build up a fake/real personality for an individual. the reason for this is to create bank accounts to be used for money laundering purposes, as they require a fake online profile to access web site that they may be banned from or to alternatively avoid the gaze and monitoring by authorities.

The methods to prevent this from happening is to firstly do not have multiple email addresses.

Secondly, do not have presences and profiles on multiple social media websites.

Thirdly, do not have multiple subscriptions to newsletter and junk email that you are not interested in. If subscribed to an email newsletter, click the unsubscribe button on the top of the email and you will be unsubscribed from the newsletter.

The less avenue that your information is available, they less like it will be used for nefarious reasons.

The use of satellite navigation systems, called satnavs, and street navigation systems for navigating around city, urban and country roads is an everyday use amongst many Individuals. This technology is now free although some subscriptions services do exist for this internet service provider. Your phone location will need to be switched on for use in navigation purposes but can remain off if only using it for viewing maps not based on current location.

Although the benefits of using such internets service provider greatly out many of the associated security concern, due care must be taken when using these applications. Never input personal and revealing information into the application such as home address, hotel name or car hire company name. When looking to navigate home or to a hotel, select an address close to your destination but not as your destination for general security reason. Also do not use voice assistance in public such as Apple's Siri or Amazon's Alexa, as this will reveal routes being taken by you in advance of taking the route. A potential assailant could lie in wait knowing that you will pass by a specific location with a mobile device and other valuables.

Never connect your sat nav to a headset as this will distract your general orientation of streets, crossing street junctions and being safe in a busy city or uncertain or new urban of country traffic. Also, if possible, avoid carry your mobile in your hand, as it is obvious to persons that are using a sat nav application and are new or visiting the area. Always plan your journey in advance even with the benefit of sat nav and avoid known areas with poor lighting, no public transport, unpopulated areas of simply areas you do not feel safe in.

A general rule of thumb is to travel in a group or in area that is tourist friendly or busy with other people. Ensure that you know what the local emergency number is and how to call emergency services from remote areas or areas with limited cell phone coverage. Never rely on internet reviews to base you decision on whether to visit a specific restaurant or tourist location. This information could be loaded and factually incorrect or worse planted by a competitor to draw you away from them in preference to an alternative location, restaurant, or service. Review website can also be geared to hotel or restaurant that offer the best discounts to the reviewing website to attract business or other forms of Hello Money. These reviews have not been independently verified and in the case of star rating for hotels this can vary from site to site depending on some unknown variable to be still explained to the customer.

Also, when planning holidays using travel sites, make sure to use reputable websites and bonded travel agents as when you start entering you expected itinerary or travel plans into a website, this information is stored immediately by the website and you will start to receive on screen pop ups and suggestive emails based on your search criteria for alternative travel plans, discounts and saving.

This maybe even if you thought you were surfing the internet anonymously without logging into an internet account. How this is done is by using internet cookies that you are required to accept when want to access a website. The type of cookies being used are quite advanced in the type of information that they collect. An internet cookie collects information about a device or user using a device and sends the information back to the website server or host server based on predefines fields of information. Cookies original function of knowing a user has previously visited a website and remembering their basic internet profile has greatly expanded beyond their remit and in some ways needs to be reined in for better internet security and transparency of information being shared with other internet enabled devices.

Interoperability of technology is where data is most likely to be compromised. This is using a port on your device to connect to another device. A port can be physical, or it can be a piece or software that listens for signals on a particular number that is addressed to that port in a piece of code.

On the internet, ports are stated in the communications between a browser and a server. So, a cyber-attack will most likely occur remotely using these ports or if code is dropped on to a device via a link clicked on or in an email attachment, then the code will generate communications from the device using a port. Most likely this will be using a different port number not intended for its defined use.

If using a hardware port on your device to connect to another device such as a peripheral device, printer, you may be using a USB cable connection. These types of connections are much less likely to be compromised than a software port, as on-site access to the device is required to establish original connection. Also, data transfer use what a called bus data connection, were data is sent using a physical hardware and instructions on your device as opposed to defined instruction which can be edited or modified in the source code.

Drivers are used to connect two pieces of hardware together. When downloading or installing drivers for a printer, only download from the manufacturer's website and from nowhere else. There are many software developers who have designed application that scan and update legacy and old drivers on your operating system. Caution should be noted with these types of applications as the locations from where updated drivers occurs is different from the manufacturers websites and sometimes it is an unknown location.

It could be the case that edited source code for drivers with a new version number is downloaded and installed on your device, giving you the impression that the driver is genuine but in fact it is a rebadged version of the manufacturer's driver with a hidden code payload. What this code contain could be anything but most likely it is source code to either keylogging you keyboard keystrokes or actively monitor and report your devices activity.

This code will also create a backdoor from where your device can be remotely accessed by a cyber hacker for nefarious reasons. These backdoors can be put into use by linking with other similarly compromised devices and creating a bot net network to take down a larger computer network that cannot be traced back to any one individual. This makes Cyber-attack stateless or geographical difficult to pin down as many actors may exist within a cyber-attack but only a few players may be pulling the actual strings.

The cost to deploy a bot net is expensive and there is a ready market for persons who want to engage in this activity with crypto currencies usually used for payment purposes, to hid nefarious activity. These botnets can usually only be used once, as their activity will be traced back to infected devices and these devices would then be blacklisted or delisted from internet activity.

Chapter 3 – Working in a Hybrid World

The workplace of the second decade in the twenty first century looks very different than it did even at the turn of the century. Today, most office-based people are solely reliant on a data connection where they can conduct their work geographically independent of the organisation head office or hub offices. People can be hired, work and resign from an organisation, never having set foot in any of the organisation's operations. They are in essence the hands and ears of an organisation, with work exclusively being conducting on the internet.

Hybrid working as it is call, means that the locations that you can work from are diverse, but still a workplace needs to feel and look like a workplace for an individual to be able to switch off at the end of the day and be able to separate their personal and work life even if both occur under the same roof.

COVID 19 legislation has allowed persons to ask for the ability to remote or hybrid work means that people who work from home or work hubs are trying mirror the ICT infrastructure that they would have in their workplace. This has caused several issues as person are buying hardware such as multi-functional devices or dual use technologies which are multi-functional printers, televisions and desktop, laptops and tablet but do not possess the technical knowledge to network these devices for their home offices.

Many bosses are rolling back hybrid working for their employees and as a result you are seeing more persons in the office for continuous days. Some of this could be put down to the simple fact of the Fear of Missing Out, and by being not in the office you might miss out on work socials, work events, new opportunities, new employments prospect or simple be disconnected from the daily events that occur in any office environment that cannot be replicated work from home or a remote location.

This Fear of Missing Out is to the benefit of bosses as they rein back in the hybrid model and were going to have to think of ways of how to get their employees back in the office who were probably originally contractually obliged to work from home or be hybrid workers.

The reasons for bosses choosing to have employees return to the office is for ease of management of staff, productivity reasons, HR policies and to easily see how the hierarchy and makeup of an organisation fits and bolds well within a single entity such as the organisations head office.

As a , most people are using the basic router sent to them by their internet service providers without any additional configuration settings or hardware. These out of the box routers were only intended for a home networking with a few Internets enabled devices and not for the kind of home network that a lot of people have nowadays. Most person will have a few devices networked without a dynamically configure firewall that adapt to new and potential harmful computer virus and cyber-attacks.

The most that a basic firewall from and internet service provider can do these days is to block all open ports on a computer and network enabled devices, which just means they stop listening for a specific network protocol. For example, such standard protocol as hypertext transfer protocol which is port 80 on a computer will be blocked by a firewall but the secure form of hypertext transfer protocol (secure) is port 443 which most firewall rules will still be enable.

It is recommended that persons who work from home upgrade their standard network devices to routers and firewall that can be configured and have more level of security functionality which can better lock down their home network, connected devices and can dynamically change setting according to new and evolving cyber threats.

Most printers come with web enabled printer functionality installed on them which means you can print document from anywhere with an internet connection. To do this you must use the printers manufactures domain specific email address. By default, this functionality is turned on at the initial configuration and setup of your printer. If left on or not properly configure this can be used as back door by cyber hackers to compromise your home network.

Most printers have a hard drive to store documents before printing. This hard drive and associated firmware for the printer does not contain any security software in any form and has a basic operating system to manage the hardware of the printer. Therefore, if a cyber hacker does compromise your home network, the best place for them to hide out is a printer. The printer can be used to monitor network activity, allow backdoor access, control network devices and update counter security patches to keep network backdoor open.

If working remotely, ask yourself the question if you really need a printer or can you use the scan function on your mobile phone and the edit and display function on you tablet for review documents interactively making notes and edits to the document as you go.

Printers' firmware, that is the operating system of the printer, has been updated very little in the last decades, making them an obvious target of any network.

Firstly, if using a printer, make sure that you give it a fixed IP, locate the printer in a separate part of your home network.

Secondly, when not is use switch it off. Do not use the power save function on the printer as a security setting thinking idle mode will not allow persons to connect to the printer.

Thirdly, most printer can print by WIFI. If this is the case, you should disable the function and only allow printing to the printer using the fixed IP address of the printer.

Fourthly, ask yourself if a document needs to be printed and that there is a business case for printing the document. Once the document is printed, there is no way to roll back access rights to the content of the document and the physical security of the document needs to be always guaranteed. If the document is no longer required, it should be shredded immediately.

Files restriction and access control. It is these case in many organisations, that no files are ever sent by as an attachment to an email. The use of email is being phased out in favour of instant messages and shared and collaboration of files in use within various collaborative software. The preference is for the implementation of access control where access to a specific file is based on a user's login credentials and the file owner can grant access to network verified accounts for a specific period. They can define the level of access and access rights that they have be it the ability to view only a file, to make edits to a file that would need to be approved by the file owners before being saved or published or reviewing the file were a member can make recommendation about file content.

This access can be rolled back, upgraded, or downgraded according to that user specific requirements at defined point of time or access revoked when no longer required to access a file. Rights access is based on the individual requirement for a specific defined and time dependent function as opposed to granting a user access to all functionality within a file, 'just in case they might need it'.

As a file owner, you need a broad range of contributors to a file, that is person who needs only to view updated or amended information, persons who add information to the file and persons who make recommendation on a course of action. This approach is reverberated around most ICT applications within the workplace.

Such example of applications that employ this file hierarchy is Microsoft One Drive and Google G Suite.

Most ICT department employ ICT security strategy called edge security which is that the edges of the network are secure for remote workers. This means as a remote worker, who may also avail of bring your own s ICT policy, you are responsible for the safety and security of you own home network and associated devices on that network.

If the edge security systems of your works' ICT department detect anomalies with devices you are using to connect to your work network, it will stop or prevent you from accessing your work network.

Edge security is part of the layered approach to an ICT department overall ICT security and cannot be circumnavigate or exceptions made for devices that have been compromised.

Most ICT departments will have a whitelist and blacklist of ICT manufactures and devices which they recommend for their network. Such manufacturer as Huawei have been blacklisted by certain companies as the firmware on their devices can be compromised and used to access networks using Huawei technologies through unofficial channels.

Home networks are also susceptible to internet prowlers. These are person who drive around areas such as the suburbs and scan the area for networks that can be compromised. This is called penetration testing but can be undertaken by anyone with a laptop. When penetration testers identify open networks with little or no security, they will note it, and this will be added to a data harvesters file on a individuals' network or online profile.

Scanning network and looking for open port can be used by downloading free software from the internet. This software scans the immediately identify areas using most used wireless protocol use in the most common types of routers. You do not need to be especially technical advanced to use these downloadable tools from the internet to identity susceptible network and scan areas and devices for vulnerabilities. In some case it is not illegal to use these types of applications. Where it does become illegal is acting on the information that you have accumulated using the free to download applications and toolkits.

Wireless peripheral devices such as keyboard and mouse are open to attacks called wireless hijacking. This is where cyber attacker will access the Bluetooth wireless protocol on your computer or laptop and try to connect to your wireless keyboard or mouse. They will also try to access the existing keyboard and mouse of your computer. What they are trying to do is to substitute their own wireless keyboard and mouse for your wireless keyboard and mouse using the Bluetooth protocol. If the cursor on you screen moves without user interaction, your device may have become compromised. If this is the case, then turn off Bluetooth on your device and use a wired keyboard and mouse. Also ensure that you device intrusion detection systems are on and functioning correctly and that your anti-virus software signature file is up to date.

There are several ways to lock down your home router.

Firstly, your home network routers should not be in a building peripheral area which will make it easier for anybody to access your home networks WIFI signal. Instead, routers should be located within the centre of you building reducing the wireless range of you WIFI network that falls outside your home.

Secondly, The SSID for your wireless network should be disabled and when search for your WIFI network to add a new device, use the routers QR code or use search by name, typing the exact SSID name for your wireless network and associated passkey in the wireless network credentials.

Thirdly, disable the DHCP server of the router and only use fixed IP address using IP V6 private addressing system for all your internet enabled device or device that are networked to you home WIFI and that do not need an internet connection such as smart devices.

Smart television also another area that are open to being compromised. These types of televisions have evolved from a cathode ray tube to plasma to lcd flat screens. These now contain the same physical types of ports found on computer monitors and laptop. This means the same technology exists on these televisions as they do on a laptop, but the firmware of television software do not contain any of the same security features that you would find on a computer. These includes a firewall, anti-virus software or intrusion detection systems. Your smart television should be connected to you home network to allow firmware upgrades to occur.

Hybrid, remote and working from home all come with their own challenges and as companies look at way to offset risk, reduce costs and improve efficiency while at the same time addressing the work life balance, the onus will turn on to everyone to address their own ICT concerns if availing or contractually required to hybrid work.

ICT department will not provide remote support to hybrid workers looking to setup their own home offices but instead standard operating procedures on device to be users and their setup, limited in scale and scope will exist. Employees may be under the impression that ICT department are obliged to provide this service but as ICT department within the organisation is a service provider and not a provisioner of ICT assets, the onus will be thus pushed back to each individual employee.

Some employees may choose to align with their own specific brand for all their ICT requirements however as addressed previously this may cause issues with security loopholes and issues that exist across an ICT hardware provider software.

This has been the case with Huawei which have allowed known back doors to exist in their routers to allow external monitoring of their devices. As a result of this compliance to their regulators in their home country, all Huawei products have been tarnished with the same brush and the market share in parts of the world has greatly reduced to the benefit of incumbent ICT providers who were initially threated and worried about cheaper imports for generic network products.

This has led to the additional issues that all electronic equipment may have intentional bugs, back doors or vulnerabilities that can be potentially exploited by third parties. As a result, their market presence and brand has been detrimentally affected to the benefit of nobody. Therefore, it is important that ICT provider choose who they get into bed with and whether this relationship is beneficial and prosperous to all those involved.

Logging into an organisation ICT Network and the method of authentication has been removed with this process being migrated to the cloud. Most large office blocks consist of shared workspace, using hot desking and faster internet connection. The phasing out of large network and photocopier printers, called multi-functional devices has also begun with persons prefer to share content with access management facility built in such as Microsoft One Drive, which can define who has access to what, what they do with the information and for how long they have access to the information.

The data connection upload and download speed is the most important aspect with encrypted traffic existing between a building, the internet, and the data centre of hosted applications. This has also removed telecoms exchanges as a hub on the internet with internet connection terminating in end of road boxes, underground or in specifically designed buildings in industrial parks.

Smart televisions are used for hybrid worker as a second screen for their computers, for teleconferencing meetings, to connect to their organisation ICT network, for research purposes and as backup device for their computers.

Smart Television are basically a problem waiting to happen and probably on a much larger scale that any botnet attack of computer virus that has plague standard desktop computers and laptops. It is therefore highly recommended that any all televisions that are connected to a home network as standard are sitting behind a firewall and bespoke router. This router should be configured by a network expert who knows how to configure a correctly for a home network and not necessarily a work network. Basic settings such as DHCP should be disabled, SSID hidden and fixed IP addresses using IP v6 used for all network enabled devices.

Television firmware should be updated whenever updates become available as they will no doubt included patches for security gaps that exist for your television. It is best to employ private networks for segregating out device traffic for your home router. Traffic routing protocol were used initially for voice over Internet protocol applications such as skype but have been adapted and evolved for other traffic heavy applications.

Many new telecoms mobile phone operators, preferring not to setup their own array of mobile base stations and cell tower choose instead as a startup to become a Mobile Virtual Network Operator, and then find a niche in the available market of focus on the demographic that their marketing department believe will gain the most market transaction.

The biggest drawn to MVNO is price which are normally are considerably cheaper than conventional mobile operator as they offer fixed monthly bundled package which includes the majority of functionality and services that an average mobile user requires.

How a MVNO work is that they buy access right to use a fixed mobile operator's cell phone tower and associated 5G network. Next the MVNO will by minutes, texts, and data bundles in large amounts from the fixed mobile provider, which are then broken out to small packages for their customers to purchase as bundle packages.

What the fixed mobile operator may do is allow the MVNO to use their 3G or 4G network while keeping access to their 5G network to their own customers. There is nothing wrong with this approach as MVNO are using tried and tested technology which otherwise would be decommissioned and no longer in public use.

If you are a user of MVNO, make yourself aware of the difference between a fixed mobile operator and a MVNO especially when it comes to customer support, which may have only limited access to the fixed mobile operators cell phone and data network.

Also when travelling, your access is at the behests of what the fixed term mobile operators agreements are in the country that you visiting and not your own MVNO agreement were they may have at one stage had separate agreements for difference counties, this approach has been abandoned due to complexity and implementation reasons, which was making it difficult to implement each agreement in different territories.

It is important before using any MVNO, to find out who's telecom infrastructure it is using to roll out is customer mobile solutions to. This may affect data privacy concerns you may have as the fixed mobile operator will have some data on you and your usage of their network based upon the logging of activity by network devices that they using to route data traffic. As such, privacy concerns that you have may have an extra hurdle to navigate and this may slow down the process if trying to ascertain the type and complexity of data that the mobile operator, be it fixed or virtual has on an individual customer.

The focus for customers for MVNO has been students and light users of mobile phone. That is Old Age Pensioners who may only make phone calls and send text messages and would not be data heavy users. Person who does not have or want to own a smart phone is another area of growth.

MVNO will normally offer mobile devices or allow other mobile phones and numbers be ported over to their MVNO network. The type of MVNO are companies that are household names and want to expand their services into other areas. There are trading on their name and reputation within an economy and as such some reputational risk does exist for these organisations.

VOIP calling is a feature that can be enabled on your mobile device, or you can use a soft phone application on your device to enable and route VOIP calls.

Most of these types of calls are encrypted and its functionality can be enabled seamlessly on your phone which removes unnecessary steps to its implementation and function. When selecting how you wish to make a call, you may have options to route a call over your mobile operator cell tower network as a voice call or a data call, through a Wi-Fi network as a data call or through a satellite network as an emergency call. If encrypting calls, make sure that if you are calling a call centre that records calls, that you are aware that such calls will not be encrypted and end to end encryption is not available in such instances unless you call using an application like WhatsApp which truncate and terminate calls which are encrypted.

Chapter 4 – Smart Everything

This chapter will look at different type of smart enabled devices and technologies both in the home and the environments that we live in. The term smart enabled devices means that it may contain sensors that can detect and relay information back to a device about real time events.

Smart homes are generally seen to be new build homes original incorporated to include structured cabling and router back to a main comms cabinet. This would be like small and medium size business. This centralised approach has all but been remove as the propensity to host data and application logic in the cloud with buildings of all sorts needing only and stable and reliable internet connection.

Nowadays, most house can be fitted as a smart home by using wireless networks as opposed to smart devices connected using structured cabling back to a patch panel. This greatly reduces the cost of deploying a smart house. As the shift of purchase moves from the network aspects to the smart enabled devices. As a result, persons who want to enable a smart home are not spending enough on network security such as a bespoke router and firewall and intrusion detection systems that is warranted for a safe and secure smart home network.

This has the resulting effect that you home and associated device that are smart enabled can be compromised from anywhere in the world using an internet connection. That means thieves do not need to be physical on site to steel your secrets and instead could open the doors and disable the security systems allowing other thieves into your home in a planned and organised robbery when you are not home.

Before you get caught up in the world of a centralise security setting for your home, like then do have in large buildings, where you can run everything in your home from one screen, this requires substantial investment, thought and design of layout before implementing. Though such devices freely available on the internet give this impression of security, know how is required in their implementation and support to make your smart home a safe and secure option.

Smart house device is freely available from internet service provider such as Google that include doorbells, alarm system and CCTV should be reviewed before purchasing. People are now buying these systems freely in DIY shops and configuring them themselves without little or no technical knowledge. This is even worse than not having an alarm or security system in your home as you are broadcasting to the world over the internet your location, whether you are home or not and other personal information for devices that are not locked down or sitting behind a firewall.

Devices, such as baby monitors, can been compromised using freely available downloadable applications from the internet. If your email address becomes compromised from a phishing attack this can have a cascading effect on your home and personal security. It is advised that you have different provider for different ICT technology may be counter intuitive, more expensive, and not using your favourite brands but division of labour is a good and simple approach to avoiding multiple systems being compromised at the exact same time.

Gmail is also a free webmail service that does not come with an instant customer service response if your account becomes compromised. Using bespoke solutions were available is much better than using free and free means open and accessible with little or no customer service.

Smart home security solutions should only be used as a layered approach to your own home security solution and should be installed by a professional. This may be more expensive approach but your home security and that of your family is what you are safeguarding in this instance and a cheap approach will only cause you problems in the long run.

A unified home security solution and network may look and seem good and practical in thinking but in one fowl swoop a cyber hacker can freely access all your home system without you even knowing it. This could go on for an indefinite period without anybody knowing as once in a cyber hack will install any security update and existing security loopholes but remain and ever-present danger to your personal security.

Smart cities are a term that used freely these days without a formal definition of what its meaning is. The basic form of a smart cities is free public Wi-Fi available anywhere within city limits which means citizens and guest can connect their devices to a free and secure and quick Wi-Fi network and thus freely communicate with each other use collaborate applications and VOIP phone calls.

What a smart city really means is that utility companies use smart enabled device to ensure energy, water, gas conservation, methods to reduce traffic congestion, better air quality by monitoring air quality and informing citizens.

Smart cities are dependent on the rollout of a complete fibre optic network throughout the city.

Green cities and smart cities can be both but follow different trajectories and strategies.

Use of real-time public transport system for mode of transport updates travel alerts and are also part of smart cities for an integrated transportation system.

All major cities and large towns now have their public transport be it trains, buses, trams or metro systems GPS enabled. This means you know exactly when your chosen mode of public transport will arrive at your stop, and the expected arrival time at your chosen designated stop as well as other information such as delays, timetable changes and strikes occurring to that route.

Note that this information can be used against an individual by a person monitoring someone's activities such as time they leave their home and arrive at work. From this they can build up you daily routine and best point and which to instigate an inception, that is a point at which they may try and apprehend you or cause you harm.

As much as they are a benefit to users of public transport and cutting down on waiting time for a mode of public transport, a degree of variation to your daily routine may be enough to sway off any potential attacker who may see you but will not engage due to this slight variation in your routine.

Smart cities are a political football as the technology to phase in aspects of smart cities are gradually phase into a city as opposed to one big bang which is a very expensive approach.

Now, complete smart cities are away off. They are being touted as new build cities in some aspects of the world but really the benefit of smart cities is to existing large and metropolis areas that have dense populations with the associated problems that go with this type of living.

Smart cities use would alleviate resource demand on the city and free up resources to be used in other aspects of a city's development. Retrofitting existing smart technologies to present day urban living is where the benefits of smart technology can really be captured. Smart cities employing technology will gradually occur over times and aspect of it are already in use such as smart grids, smart and unified public transportation systems and interoperability of function and technology remove single use functionality from a city.

Many grant are available to make use of a houses roof space for solar panel and electricity generation. These devices should not be attempted for self-install as they require electricity conversion from dc to ac and power storage using batteries.

Electricity that is not immediately used is stored and can be sent back into the grid and at agreed upon rate with your electricity provider. This energy saving conservation approach should be part of you overall approach to reducing your carbon footprint.

At no point should your solar panel array ever been connected to your home network. This will likely invalidate your contract with your energy provider as a provider, will open the grid to potential cyber-attack, illegal under various legislation and highly irresponsible.

The reason for this is obvious. You are connecting two utility service providers together at a point down the line were little or no monitoring is going on.

As a result, a spike in electricity may inadvertently travel down and up both utility providers network and damage or destroy various aspects of the network. Most data networks backbone is copper as copper can easily transmitted electricity signals. The fundamental of digital signal and the underbelly of the internet and digital device is an on/off state which is the same as electricity as it is potentially in use in either an on or off state.

Joining these networks will therefore allow electricity and electrical loads greater than intended to flow through the networks. Even though a lot of coppers networks have been upgraded to fibre optic connection which is better able to prevent such occurrence from occurring, there is still the potential for a power spike to occur.

Fibre optic networks work using the transmission of light signal containing data through cables. The bundles of cable allow a greater throughput of signal and data along a cable. If at any point the cable fails, then the whole cable will fail. With copper cable you only must worry about the one sheathed cable with fibre cable this has greatly increased.

How this effects our internet security is the same as wiretapping, were listening devices were placed on a person's telecom line and carried signal were listen to. With fibre cables this is exactly what happens, but instead of it happening to one individual on a street were a court order probably has been obtained, instead what you are having is the known collection of data by the large internet companies. This happen at browser level and logic level, that is the information you populate into the search box, network level, how internet traffic is relayed and server level, from which device the requested information is stored and what internet address requested.

Smart watches and other assistive technologies such as smart phones now have many functionalities that can be used to monitor your health, daily activities and reporting back to you about trends, and concern that may warrant further investigation by a doctor or specialist. These features can be beneficial to your overall health and well-being and ensure you are getting adequate exercise or sleep. These types of features are user dependent and requires user to turn these features on and actively monitor the information that your phone or smart watch is generating.

The smart watches features, or smart phone make suggestion based on parameter enters in about the users age, sex, weight, and other demographic information as using various data mining algorithms, artificial intelligence algorithms to draws a comparison to individuals with similarly entered demographics.

As a result, this approach is not an exact science and should be seen as an aid not a replacement to your chosen health professional. The information can be shared with defined persons.

Ensure that if you are sharing this information that the entered demographic information is correct and in real time. That includes your weight, prescribed medication and sleep times which require reaffirming estimates so that information shared makes as much sense as possible to person reviewing this raw data.

These features can be used as part of agreed health and weight management program with your doctor, dietician, or other medical profession. These applications use sensors and GPS to ascertain information such as pulse rate and type of exercise as opposed to a smart phone that will catch you gait and steps count.

There is a difference between passive data collection using various sensors and enter data which can be parse with collected data to build up an overall picture of your activities, health and general well-being which may require you to enter in information periodically about yourself and well-being. Therefore, merging this information will give a better picture of you overall health.

The major data concern with this data capturing is that you are aware of the type of information being captured, where this information is stored and that there is no information leakage to online data sites by allow applications with online features access to this personal information.

It is prudent to review access rights of applications you have granted permission to access data to on your digital devices. Be aware if you grant access to an application on one device this may inherit is access rights to the same application and user account on another device.

Any health-related information should have a written agreement with your health or medical profession so both parties agree what information you are sharing, the reason for this information being shared and how long this information is to be shared. You should also state what will happen to this information once the agreed time range capture has expired.

Also remember this information always captures your location and activity, so maybe you only want to share information based on a certain activity or time.

Electric cars and their associated management devices can be easily compromised as the on-board computer can be wireless enabled for diagnostic reason, for artificial intelligence reason such as driver assist or for energy consumption tracking.

It is recommended that under no circumstances should your electric car be connected to any wireless network through your mobile phone. If connecting your mobile phone or tablet to your electric car, do not enable and open an accessible internet connection. That is do not use the 5G network of your mobile provider or do not allow your mobile device to connect to a wireless network. This could void any warranty that exists for your electric car.

Separation and segregation of technology is always a simple safeguard for multiple interfacing devices.

Also at publicly available charge stations, do not allow you e-car to be compromised by only using official an authorised e-charging stations. Unofficial charging stations setup for varying reasons could damage the battery and electrics of your car.

Check your e-car manufacturers list of authorized charging stations before embarking on a long journey. Remember a log file of each charging station that you use is kept by your e-cars memory chip and that of the charging station as well as that of the manufacturer of your e-car.

This information is used to ascertain such statistic as average distance achieve before recharging, gaps in e-charging networks and technical issues with on board navigation systems.

E-cars are in the process of replacing all fossil fuel enabled modes of transportation and as a result cars are a good mechanism to trial new technologies before rolling out on more heavy-duty vehicles.

Certain technical advances may occur in a relatively short period of time which means that you e-car should be regularly checked by a registered e-car mechanic and not by you or an e-car enthusiasts.

E-cars are not toys and as such should be serviced in the same manner as you would a fossil fuel enabled vehicle.

Chapter 5 – Data Content Creators and the Internet

Structured cabling approach using cat5e or cat 6 is seen as a very expensive approach to network enabling a building. The use of wireless technology both inside buildings and in public has greatly reduced the barrier of entry for internet related activities for individuals of all shape and size to be able to get on the internet in a very substantial way.

Internet Services Providers are inadvertently introducing traffic tiering unbeknownst to internet users. This approach takes the shape of upload and download speeds which in essence is not factually correct. Fibre connections only have one speed, however traffic can be throttle at node point and traffic routing or traffic separation points. This means that traffic is prioritised for organisation who require their service to be delivered quickly and speedily.

This service is not written into contracts but instead offered to organisations based on several factors. Such organisations include stream service providers, advertising delivery providers and content delivery service providers. These areas of the economy are highly competitive and there is a general demand and expectation that these service providers service quick, speedily and does not disconnect when streaming content.

Ever noticed when streaming content, your internet connection may drop for some unexplained reason even though you may be directly connected to your home internet router using the LAN function of the router. This is because if your internet connection runs through a standard telephone exchange, and there are limited number of internet ports available at any one time. If too many calls are made at the same time to these banks of internet port, just like traffic on the road you will first get a slower connection speed and after a period the telecom exchange will notice this and just like dropping a call will drop your internet connection, that is the persistent connection between your router and the local telephone exchange.

As a result, your router will have to reestablish the internet connection with the telephone exchange by calling it until it finds a free internet port. The time it takes to find a free internet port can vary greatly and this time is known as down time, that is you do not have an internet connection.

So, the internet is now a tiered service based on business interests and not for the general good of humanity for the sharing of knowledge as the original founders of the internet intended it for. This means that the type of information easily accessible, especially with the onset of artificial intelligence, will be in type, topic and interest with research, development and human evolution being pushed to the back of the internet queue with movies, tv channels and video streaming sites taking priority.

The monetising of the internet was always inevitable and the dot com bubble of the early part of this century was an illustration of what the internet was capable of, but early adopters were just that, way too early to the party with nothing new to offer. The research and development by investment vehicles only started paying off when the likes of the big seven internet companies of that Amazon, Google and Facebook started generating quarterly income in the billions with their only footprint being data centres and offices. No brick-and-mortar shop, no production capacity and no distribution network and centres, yet these companies were valued a lot more that companies that organically grew and who were decades older.

Streaming services will eventually replace traditional broadcasting television channels and distribution as the upkeep of this distribution service is too expensive to maintain. Most of the business models that use traditional broadcasting services are owned or managed by state and are seen as representing the national interest of a country. They are seen as holy grails and should be not interfered with. But customer demand is wanning for broadcasted, real time and live service in preference to on demand streaming services.

Customers want to view the content they want at a time that is convenient to them and not the broadcaster. Simple things as the main news being latter in the evening does not make sense in the twenty first century with news readily available 24 hours a day when they want. Breaking news is just that instead of waiting for a news flash, new bulletin, special bulletin, and scheduled news time to bring a story that is to the general interest of the public.

How we digest information has changed. How we interpret data is also changing and our attention span is also changing. Stories should be crisp, precise, to the point and factually correct. Fake news and deeps fakes are just a blimp in the information age and new techniques have been deployed to remove fake news from distribution sites.

Deep fakes are generated using artificial technology applications and as such markers are inserted in these artificial Intelligence machines that are used to detect fake or regurgitated news or spliced news. That is news stories that have been pieced together from other bits of news stories.

So, when news is delivered straight away the chances of it being used in fake news is less and less likely. It will become the case that news will be the job of every citizen of a country and not left to the few.

News stores could be uploaded to a verified and reputable site, screen and then published. The interest lies in who access the website, monetising websites and how professional these websites are hosted and managed. Free public broadcasting services have been limited in growth for these reason as democracy is based freedom and accuracy of speech. Backing your words with actions has been limited to the interest to organised protest and boycotts based on the interest of platform they serve.

The type of services that can be monetised on the internet are similar in scope and focus on selling products and services. Gting beyond this point is the next growth for the internet. How to make money from something other than a product or service. As a result, internet growth will loop and focus on a few companies and industries that swallow up smaller companies and become behemoths in the area that they focus in on.

Internet subscription services. Internet service provider operate a subscription service which is normally monthly with an initial free trial period. Many people sign up to subscriptions service based on the initial free trail period and never review their own business case for the subscription. This means they may have never had a reason to signed up for the service in the first place, if there are already signed up to an existing similar service, if they are on the correct price tier, if the number of devices enabled matches the price tier that they are on, and if data breaches with the subscription services has occurred.

This may affect their trust in the service. It is important to review all subscriptions services that you have signed up to. If you do not know which service you are a paid subscription member of, then review your bank statement for your monthly out goings. Try to match direct debit mandate names against that of the subscription service as most time they are not the same name. This is additional confusion and another ploy by internet service providers to prevent you from cancelling any subscription service. It is the anticipation that subscription services that you have signed up as a paid customer, you will not question the reason in the first place. If in doubt about what service you have really signed up for, cancel the subscription and if you really need the service, you will be able to sign up again without any hidden cancelation fees or joining fees.

There are several streaming giants in the marketplace that have similar offerings; select one for your household as the content is normally over lapping with similar movie and television shows available from differing streaming platforms. Where exclusivity content exists, use the pay per view model and only paid for the content that you want to watch.

Other types of subscription services include anti-viral software. Most operating systems now have an anti-virus application in built along with other security application. Make sure you are not paying for a subscription anti-virus application that you don't , or worst still is affecting the performance of your computers operating system. An anti-viral application that is native to your computer rather than an installed application is a much better option as it allows for integration of applications installed on your computer.

Although the number of satellites being sent into orbit has never been more and the speed of sound to light equalising equation curve has been smoothen and transmission delays lessened, it is hard to see where the demand for growth exists or will exist. Distance is time and even using low orbit array satellites is still expensive and time consuming for transmission of a signal. The faster distance between two points is not always a straight line and using a satellite to bounce a signal off, amplify and relay on which is essential what a satellite and satellite array is, is not the most efficient way to transmit a signal.

Persons using satellite phone and satellite broadband always complain about cloud cover effecting either the ability to make a phone call and to access the internet. Some satellite providers try to use the naturally curvature of the planet to relay signals at a faster speed. This new and novel approach is using a combination of ground transmission stations and satellites to find the most efficient and safest route between two points. The word safest in this content means that data is not physically moving through areas of the world that are geologically sensitive and where data could be intercepted for pollical reasons.

As a result, you should always query where any information that you save to the cloud is stored, were any application logic is processed and routes taken by your data connection to hosted applications in data centre. One overlooked fact that is not addressed by most employers is the route taken by an employee's home internet connection to an organisations data centre of hosted application data, as most employees believe once you reach an internet backbone it is irrelevant.

However, internet service provider using various real time generated routing algorithms to route internet traffic based on a predefined priority list. This traffic routing also called traffic tiering has been in existence since commercial sold data connections have been available and paying for a guaranteed data port on a bank of modems, ISDN connection or ADSL connection meant a faster data connection to your nearest telephone exchange.

But since incumbent telecom provider charge deregulated entities cost to access and install equipment as well as rent in their telephone exchanges, it has become a lot cheaper for new media companies to run their own fibre lines and termination points. This has been duplication of fibre lines in commercial heavy parts of a city resulting in unnecessary road digging and road works. A single telecoms company will thus fibre the most profitable parts of a city and leave the rests on a standard copper cable.

So, deregulation has resulted in some positive gains, some negative points and some battlefronts and price undercutting to gain market traction. What this means to you as a customer of a media company is that eventually you will have a similar setup to a railway system, were one large company will start buying media companies to have a regional fibre optic network exclusively for their customers. Anyone else wanting to use this fibre optic network will have to buy time in chunks and then resold as smaller packages to individual customers. The reason for this is like any new product, cost will come down over time due factor such as availability, market share and competition.

As a result, consolidation is always a factor. Most fibre optic networks have been also future proof to support data traffic and connection of greater speed and throughput. So, in essence you have an underutilised network yet to fully realise its true potential. This obviously means increased revenue for any and exiting owners of such networks. That is why the question of increased deployment of satellite arrays remains a mystery.

The next question about the internet and data connectivity is application logic. One of the main reasons for using hosted applications provider is that the application logic is store in the cloud and any new updates occur at server level and not local area network or device level. This means that any downtime of the application due to updates being applied is the responsibility of the application service provider and not any organisation that is a customer of that application service provider.

With that data hosting is also the responsibility of the application service provider. This in time will most likely revert where data will return to an on-premises form and application logic will be hosted on the cloud. This application logic will be parsed with on-site stored data with the resulting information only being displayed and available in a viewable form in an on-site location.

The analogy is like a coffee maker with the coffee being the application logic and the filter being the on-site data with the resulting information being created as an output. To make sense of the data you would not only need the raw data, but the application logic views specific to an organisation to make any sense of the data.

There you would need administrative access to two different silos of separately but related functionality. From a data security perspective, this approach makes sense and in only functionality is using the internet for accessing essence forms and not data. This means that data breaches can only occur due to human factor and not necessarily from technical reasons.

The analogy would be like being in a house but only every being in one room at a time in that house and moving from one room to another requires opening and closing one door to another.

As a user of these types of systems greater granularity and access control would exist with persons tasked as experts in one specific functionality of an application without understanding or seeing the full functionality, complexity, or logic of the application.

Streaming or downloading. The best approach to video or audio content from the internet is to stream as opposed to downloading content. With this you do need a persistent and stable internet connection for streaming were for downloaded content you can watch offline when required. By streaming content this means that content is downloaded from the internet for one time view and then you forget about that this content is on your device hard drive which is just taking up space.

Also, some downloadable content may be only viewable for a short period of time and then not viewable also unnecessarily taking up hard drive space. Ensure that when purchasing internet content that you do have the right and correct licence to view content. Also ensure that when accessing content outside your native country that you do have the rights to view content. If not do not, then don't view this content as you will be breaking international laws and regulations.

Content compression applications. Many content that comes in video, audio or as a still photograph has been compressed to save space and make it easier to send files and attachments over the internet. Many of these formats you would have heard such as jpeg and mpeg. However, some of these compression applications can hide hidden content and objectives.

For example, code payloads can be stored in with mpegs and jpegs images and when accessed or opened using an application on your device, may inadvertently cause the hidden source code to run and install whatever function the source code has been designed to do. The only safe way to view content sent to you over the internet is to use your anti-virus software installed on your device to scan files before being viewed. This will check for anything unusually with or within a file or attachment. This could save your device from becoming infected with a virus that could corrupt system files or block you from accessing your device all together.

Napster, Tor network using Onion router and pier to pier file sharing. Before streaming became a feasibility possibility for internet users, there was pier to pier file sharing where anybody who downloaded an application like Napster essentially turning their computer into a file sharing server accessible to anybody on the internet.

If you wanted to download a pirated version of a file, you would search and find the best connection with a complete copy of the file and you would then be put in a queue to the download file. If the server went offline or dropped the connection, then you would be directed to another version of the file available on the internet or simply waited for the file server to come back online.

As a result of this approach to using TCP/IP, Microsoft removed network discovery protocol and file sharing in its existing form from its operating system.

You had people sharing files from the root C drive of their computer beside system files for Microsoft of other essential system files. This was in days that internet security and cyber security was nothing like it is today. Even to think about doing something like that today would be not only illegal but would make you device susceptible to all known computer hacks and viruses.

But this is how applications that we use today for our everyday tasks evolved from a client only setup to a client server setup by simple switching on the file sharing protocol on a client computer.

Nowadays, faster internet connections and the phasing out of dial up connections to connect to the internet means this type of approach is not relevant to the average user but to those who wish to compromise your devices. However, most device firewalls and intrusion detection systems would spot this type of activity on your computer and either alert you to this activity on your device or shut it off to prevent your computer from being compromised.

Music streaming sites like Spotify and Amazon music means you do not need to purchase or download music but instead stream from a library of database of music. In instances where you do download music, music is generally stored by the applications library you downloaded in a format that is specific to the library or application or the website. As a result the amount of music that people actually own or physically have on their device has been greatly reduced within the last two decades from 100% were all music even if stored on a digital library would have a physical copy of that album or song, to some below 50% or less today were music is mainly purchased and stored within the music library of a music provider and never leaves the server of the music provider.

This has serious ramifications for ownership of music as in reality you do not own the music you own but are renting its use for the time you have a subscription to that music service. If music is purchased and downloaded, you will find it difficult to transfer or move the music from one digital library to another or one music device to another.

Eventually music will only be available by streaming with no ability to own or download the music to a device. As a result, you will need a persistent internet connection to access and listen to music. As a result of this strategy by the music industry, you are seeing a revolt by music enthusiasts back to the days of music on vinyl and tapes which allowed people to play the music of their choice and taste as opposed to what is available on a streaming services digital library.

This has certainly given the music industry and the general information technology industry some reason to rethink that music is not necessarily about ease of use but instead giving the audience what they want based on their taste in music. As a result, the music industry is having to take a step back a in some cases back to its routes of where they originated from and retrace what went wrong in the customer surveys and market research as to where public interest lies in music.

For the wider Information technology sector, subscription services, on demand or always available content may have reach a maturity level and review is now needed as to how the monetization of content is occurring. If we start seeing a renewed interest in bricks and mortars stores which seemed to have been on a slow march to death for a long time based on ecommerce websites and a new supply chain based on a large fleet of delivery vans, then we know that the information technology industry has taken a step to far and not is giving the customer what they wants but instead tried to second guess what the customer will like, long before that became an idea in most people minds.

This is a dangerous pre-emption to take as you're a feeding the customer something they don't know that they don't want. The major factors effecting the bricks and mortar store was not ecommerce but covid-19 lockdowns and the inability to open for customer requirements. But the rebound from Covid-19 and associated spending bubble from savings has spawned a new generation of bricks and mortar stores well beyond coffee shop and restaurant to on street gyms, yoga classes, alternative medicine and other types of business that were not seen in the main street of a town or cities but instead were built on cheaper and marginal lands of a town. So, trends will change our spending habits and daily routine.

Chapter 6 – The Darker Web

The internet is a borderless network that is locked down by service provider based on Internet address. What this means is that you cannot access a service based in another country for price disparity reasons. Some people use what is called proxy servers to reroute their internet traffic making it look like an internet connection is coming from a specific location by routing traffic through a local server. This is not a practise that you should engage in as it will come to the surface with your Internet Service Provider and any illegal activity in your immediate area may be thought to come from your proxy server connection. There is little recourse to this action as the action is illegal and traffic is generally encrypted by the proxy servers. Saying that it was not you may have little or no meaning and little or no ability to prove your innocence.

The dark net which was the underworld of the internet has been largely brought to the mainstream, accepted and in some instances, practises legislated in the legal framework of its society and thus to its acceptance. As a result, the dark under bellow of human activity is no longer anonymous or unknown.

The dark net was largely subdued when the founders of the web site, Silk Road, were exposed, arrested, trialled, and sentenced. The thinking was that the dark net would go further, and further underground as would be the case with any underground activity, but this has not been the case. The reason for this is that the creator of silk road and similar websites where in essence acting in the best interest of organisations that they are working for. Not to put too fine a point on it they worked for organisation whose currency for their operations was working with activities associated with such sites as Silk Road. Nowadays buying banned items on the internet does not require a central website but simply can be done using what's app messaging service. Even though such applications are , these applications can be easily manipulated to transmit information cloaked, hidden or coded. No drama, no fuss.

However, content can be uploaded in a different jurisdiction without any technical or legal recourse and simply been shared out to internet users. Once content is on the internet it is very difficult to kill it. The reason for this is the legacy use of proxy servers and cache server as well as freeness or cheapness of online data storage facility which allows user free storage up to 5 GB of data without the need for a subscription account.

Although a verified internet account is required, the word verified only means that you verify using a web email service which does not need to be verified. It seems that internet service providers are playing pass the parcel when it comes to verification of the identities behind internet accounts.

This could be a similar issue to that of twitter which overestimated the amount to verified accounts it had when looking the be bought out. When it came to verifying the user accounts it had, it seemed that many were bot accounts setup for advertising and monetisation reasons and they were controlled by companies looking to inflate users' profiles by the number of followers they have, the amount of likes they got for a post or the spread of demographics that was following a specific profile. These sock puppet accounts, the name originating from children's programmes where a hand under the table controlled a sock puppet, are accounts control by third parties and not real accounts with a real person identity.

These services can be bought by web site owners, you tube channels content provider and others in the same space to manipulate their viewing audience numbers. As opposed to television viewership which is conducted globally by a company called Nielson were amount of viewership to television content through a transmission network is strictly monitored and these numbers have a direct impact on advertising spending, no such process exists for content delivered either downloaded or streamed on the internet.

For video and music streaming services the numbers of downloads or stream of a song, movie or tv show cannot and is not independently verified. What investors are concerned about is churn rates and subscriber numbers and spending per user account. So, the metric of viewership or listenership has been in essence dropped as an important metric for the viewing of online content.

This raises several questions as to why an individual metric, which is embedded as a metric for demographics to a television service has not migrated as an important if not the gold standard of metric for online content which it is for traditional broadcast television services.

As such this metric has been hijacked by any internet user for their own benefit and allows the room to exist for organizations to setup and provide the facility to inflate and boost a website or online channels overall viewership and rating.

This means sites on hosted server farms can use varying methods to modify their actual numbers but if you look at the web site internet traffic you will see a big difference. So, a data centre specifically hosting websites may have very little internet traffic, but online reporting mechanisms may paint a completely different message.

Fake sock puppet accounts can also be used for harmful reasons. It is normal for people to want to dress up as something that is different to their normal make up or personality. This can happen at Halloween, for black tie parties, for pride parades, musical festivals, and other events. This allows people to break away from their conventional thinking for a time and act completely different to the way they would in the normal world. As such we are creating an alternative profile or persona to the one that we normally inhabit. This can be especially seen in the music scene. However, this need to alternate has create a dark and more dangerous side to are society.

CAPITAL OF SPIES

This is where the cross over from fun to personal pleasure goes to a whole new level. What it is, persons who prey on the young and vulnerable of our society for their own gain and enjoyment. This activity can start as persons of a greater age trying to engage with a young person through the internet. As with any internet activity that we feel is dangerous or threating to our society or our way of life, we need to view, review and report. In any society, preying on the young and vulnerable is not tolerate in any form, so safeguarding our children activity on the internet should avail of operating systems features and functionality.

Proxy servers are used by individuals to connect to foreign or banned services and to also hide their internet IP address. If you find out that someone you know or live with is using a proxy server, ask what they are using the proxy server for. It maybe to watch content that is not available in their own country.

However, this circumnavigating rights restriction is illegal and could cause you to be fined by internet service provider for someone else's internet activities. What a proxy server will do is provide the content server with a local IP address that will make content available to that IP addresses which is then routed back to another IP address using the proxy service. So, you are telling the content server, yes, I am resident of this country, and I am allowed to access this content, when in fact you are not a resident of the country and are in fact a national from a foreign country accessing internet services and associated content without a license to view or access that content.

When you read it like that, as the way the courts would see and interpret it, it shows you that it is not some harmless internet activity but something far more serious and dangerous. At a minimum your home IP address will be blacklisted, next your home country Internet Service Provider maybe contacted, and details given of internet activity conducted on the content servers view list. Your ISP may issue you with a warning, may take a legal route which would be to contact police for further investigation. You may be banned from traveling to the country in questions as well as several escalation points that can and do occur. Do not get trapped in a situation like this based on the reason that you want to view a yet to be released movie or television show not available to you. It could have far more serious ramifications.

Dodgy boxes. For many years there was ways to get subscription satellite televisions services without having to pay the monthly subscription or setup costs. This way was to get what is called a dodgy box installed and connected to your television. What this does is it uses a standard media subscription service, unscrambled the satellite images using constantly changing codes that must be entered in daily or weekly or whenever the satellite company changes its signal.

How this is allowed to happen is an inside job. As satellite subscriptions, anyone can pick up the scrambled signal as opposed to IPTV or streaming services where you need a subscription account to access the streamed service signal. The signal is broadcasted through satellites and ground relay signal stations. At these ground relay stations; a backdoor has been allowed to exist that allows the signal to be transmitted descrambled once you have the correct access code.

Obliviously the satellite and content providers are losing a lot of money by this back door existing to their premium services and it has become difficult for these companies to close these open relays as they can be moved to another relay station. It is no doubt that transmitting data using satellite for commercial purposes will be phased out as the speed and cost of over land fibre cables and fail over and redundant to this connection becomes much cheaper and easier to manage.

Content sharing platform. The internet has many contents sharing platform used to generate income for individual. The main one being YouTube. Here people monetize their content through vlogs, videos and audio content hosted by google. Remember the adage, don't believe everything you read, but in this context don't believe everything you see.

There are videos on the internet containing deep fake, which are where the video and person or context in the video has been edited, modified, or doctored to get you to believe that such a person said or did something. This is not always the case and data harvesters could have easily lifted a person profile picture from their social media profile and used it by cropping the picture over another person face, making you think that such a person was the actual person in the video.

Some deep fakes are easy to spot as it is obvious that the head of the person does not match their body and vice versa. However smarter deep fakes use artificial Intelligence algorithm to better match or marry the two photographs together. As such these images, be it stilled photographs or videos are much more difficult to spot. As such the deep fake can be used to create or increase traffic to a website and increase revenue to a website based on click through, likes and shares.

So, this an ulterior reason for employing deep fake this as opposed to setting out to damage an individual's reputation, career, or social standing.

The best way to get your news is from media outlets that would be greatly affected using deep fake contained in their media outlets. These are normal subscription service news provider who may have pay walls, a subscriber base, or high-profile advertisers.

If an advertiser suspects that deep fakes are being used by a media outlet to generate traffic, then they will normally instigate an investigate themselves and if warranted cancel an advertising contract that they have with the media outlet. This is to protect their reputation and if necessary, the reputation of who the deep fake is about if a person in the political or social scene within a country or and internet or international celebrity.

Deep fakes may be a sign of the times, but fake news is nothing new and has been around for centuries. As such we must be wary and form our own opinions based on sound and verified information before judging those being trialled by the media.

Chapter 7 – The future of Artificial Intelligence and Data Privacy

Artificial Intelligence is a topic that has caught the attention of media, the public and various organisations around the world, but it is nothing new and has been an area of computer science research since at least the sixties. Its current definition is quite broad but what it is about is trying to make some useful from large amounts of data. The data has caused the creation of huge data centres for the sole purpose of storing and sharing information. As a result, organisation asked themselves if they can make better use of this information using prove areas of computer science research.

Artificial intelligence has nothing to do with robots and process automation which are also separate areas of research for computer scientists.

What artificial intelligence is the application of data algorithms to defined data set with defined parameters for find patterns and repetition. From this we create data models from which we apply data sets to train these data models around the data. So, it's like tailoring a suit. The persons initial measurements are taken, then a suit is made from these measurements and finally and fitting at which alterations are made for a final fit. Drawing pins are used to keep alterations made into place.

In essence this is what artificial intelligence. At the end we get a tailored suit based on the initial measurement taken and alterations made at fitting of suit.

So, the outcome of artificial intelligence is wholly based on the information we provide to the data algorithms been trained. In this case the trained outcome is information based on inputs.

How Artificial intelligence interacts with us current is either try assistants on our phone such as Sir and on our home network like

Alexa. How they act is they train their algorithms to your voice and upon voice commands respond to tasks provided.

Also, we may see chatbot and applications like ChatGPT and Microsoft Co-pilot for edge which respond by providing text for defined questions and set parameters.

In the area of privacy, it has seen around the world where various ICT hardware providers have aligned themselves with their home countries regulatory authorities to gain government contract, curry favour with those in power, increase market share reason and access to foreign markets, to satisfy regulatory demands such as specific network features, operating systems, and system settings in countries around the word. This practise has come to the fore such case as Huawei and this practise is not only confined to this company. Serious questions have been asked about the safety and security of these devices with many countries choosing to ban there use for any type of network within their country.

The reason for this is that all network enabled devices require a unique identity to distinguish itself from other devices on a network or on the internet. If this IP address which is either public or privately facing is release, then it is easy to know your location and various ways can then be used to access your network.

Mac addresses have been replaced in essence with IP Version , previously IP version 4, which has led to the greater expansion of the internet.

How we manage our own personal internet security comes down to the information we know and the information we have access to. Value is no longer associated with applications, devices, or network connectivity but instead the data layer of an application.

Artificial Intelligence will only prove this assumption correct as artificial intelligence applications can only generate new content based on new inputs. In essence they fill in the blanks of content using data libraries based on context and frequency of use. The more use a sentence, paragraph or article is referenced, the more times aspects of this data will appear in other content.

The outcome will be content banks like land banks, where information will be stored not for immediate use but either to take is out of use or to find a use that can be monetised at a later stage. These content banks are governments who are the largest hoarders of data in history.

Information that government have, control and own is unchecked and unmonitored. The thought that any government has ever deleted any information on a citizen is nonsensical and a joke. Even where legislation exist to protect individuals' privacy this law has been circumnavigated by rehousing information in different jurisdiction, compartmentalising information or information substitution and splitting where information is stored not in contiguous lines of information but broken up into illogical text to the extent that they are deemed to be meta data.

This information is yet to find a use but no doubt the recent renewed interest in the computer science research area of artificial intelligence which has been mainstream area of research since the sixties will be one area that meta data will be pointed at to see what can happen. This will unfortunately result in something that resembles the property and subprime mortgage crash of 2008. This is where money, meets research meets sound fundamental beliefs to create a short pop but long flop.

The only people that will benefit from such an arrangement is the internet companies who will take investment from the likes of hedge fund and financial institutes who believe they are representing the best interests of their customers and clients. As such billions have already been invested in the black hole funds with little or no oversight. This means that this will cause investment to be focused in area beneficial to parts of society who believe the future of mankind exists with robots and artificial intelligence and not addressing the pressing issues of global change, break down in democracy and civil order and the general well-being of our fellow citizen.

Large organisations will address the obvious corporate social responsibility gap by funding shovel ready projects located in poor in city areas, aftereffects of natural disaster cause by global warming or publishing research which they claim will cause them to refocus their business interest to the mutually benefit of society. Plastering over the cracks with little or no long-term benefit just to save face.

Monies are now being focused on areas within computers seen to generate growth based on artificial factors and real-world realities. The outcome of artificial intelligence research will be sameness in that data and data points will merge at a similar point and decisions will be based on computer data and not real-world experiences. Information feed into artificial intelligence algorithms could be easily manipulated to given false positives, untrue outcomes, and factual inaccurate data sets.

As a result, the creator and designer of these artificial intelligence algorithms are essence the future decision makers of our world and not elected official and person employed to perform such roles. This could cause issues with the general of our world as decision making process will completely be taken out of the hands of those who are required to act in any functioning democracy.

What the future looks like rings very true to movies. Large corporations and not government running the world based on the need for resources. Artificial Intelligence is just a tool to allow this to happen. It is equivalent to removing air from a room and then selling it back to a person for money. It wasn't theirs's to own in the first place but some they now are a monopoly to themselves for this vital resource and nothing can be do as legitimate means were used to gather this essential resource.

We are now at a crossroads in how the internet is to develop in the coming decade. Do we allow it to simply be used as a digital marketplace for goods and services, a platform for data sharing and exchange or does it hold a higher objective yet to be discovered or unlocked. This could be its use leads to the complete removal of currency and value from our civilisation. Some theories extend to people bartering their services online in exchange for goods or services. Personal development and education would be conducting on the internet freely without any requirement for payment, subscription, or value. This would leave space and time for people to freely develop at their own pace and time without pressure from external stimulus or persons.

We would have a civilisation that is culturally deep, skills adept and hopefully a more happy and inclusive society. How this would develop in the initial stages is yet hard to fathom, however this approach does already exist in practise. The only thing holding back its development is preconceived belief about life, how it should be lived and what we are living for. These philosophical questions may not need to be answered at all but instead a breakdown of previous beliefs need and their removable as a viable option for growth.

Privacy is something as an individual we all appreciate. However, in some quarters it is becoming a luxury that is for the marginalised of our society. That is more ingrained your identity is in any society the more unlikely you are going to enjoy some level of privacy. What these means if you are a homeless person in the street, the most public you can be, you are likely to not generate much interest in you but if you are going around you daily task, every aspect of your movement will either be followed by your mobile device, CCTV, drones, and other people's mobile devices.

The accumulation of data to be processed for various reasons such as security, design of cities, movement of persons and other reason means that people's privacy are being infringed upon daily for greater good of some greater purpose. However, we are all guilty. How many times do we accept new terms and conditions for use of an internet service provider without reading what exactly we are agreeing to.

Amongst this text, lies all the answer to our privacy concern but we readily accept these terms and as thus have very little legal course once knowingly accepting these terms. It seems there is a little of sacrifice of privacy to use these free internet services.

Privacy may be a word that only existed in the past as now every aspect of our planet is monitored in some way shape and form, either actively or passively. Every bit of data that is created is stored somewhere either in hard or soft copy for legal purposes or to be retrieve later. The insertion legal guidelines and legislation is a piece token form or appeasing civil right activists who claim and correctly claim that privacy is dead not just redefined into an evolved form that goes hand in hand with human evolution. So, maybe we are right just to click and accept new terms and conditions for internet services because, privacy is for the very poor not the very rich.

Chapter 8 – Identity Theft and ICT Security

Internet security because of how the internet has grown has greatly changed throughout the last two decades as the number of Internet enable devices has greatly increased, internet hosted content has greatly increased, and the number of data connections has greatly increased.

Internet security has moved from on site to co-location to hosted security solutions. The trend is no doubt moving from a centralised approach to a decentralised approach or distributed according to devices. This is sometimes referred to the internet of thing which is saying that all electronic devices will be chipped, and network enabled. There is certainly a movement against this thinking for security reasons and sovereignty of a state where private industries may hold greater influence and power over a state than its elected government.

Interoperability of devices running different operating systems has been created with standard internet protocols being used. The internet by its foundation requires the use of commonly agreed internet standard, protocols, and approaches for all these differing technologies to work.

Identity theft is an increasingly important area of security concern for internet companies. The removal of password sharing for streaming sites was internet content provider addressing identity theft in a softly approach, without raising eyebrows amongst its customers. This policy removed the ability of multiple users sharing the one streaming account. As a result, users require their own profile for streaming content.

This is also addressed adverting bounce, where advertising based on users' demographics is delivered to the wrong users due to a different person viewing the content from that of the account holder. The concept of using accounts is that one person is assigned an account and is the only user of that account. Streaming service have also beefed up their security with the introduction of multi factor authentication for user accounts as standard. This process is also tied to one user mobile phone number, like WhatsApp, and as a result possession of an authentication device is required in order access streaming content.

Using your bank card. Using tap and go and chip and pin enabled cards comes with some hidden security risks. If an amount is over a certain value or if you have used tap a go three times in a row you will be required to enter your card pin. Make sure to cover the terminal when entering in your pin. If you see people intentional hanging around an epos terminal and trying to view a user's pin, what they are trying to do is to clone you card and get your card pin to have unrestricted access to processing transactions using your card. This practise is quite common. What this means is that they have epos which can clone bank cards. These people may know your favourite hangout, takeout or restaurant were you regular make purchases.

As such they know more about you then you may realise and at the first instance of spot this trend, do not think your being paranoid, do not tell a friend to ask for their advises as it is your own senses and opinions that are alerting you to this potential threat and not anybody else. You are just as good judge or character as anybody else to this type of activity. It is recommended that you change your daily routine, where you shop and spend and how you communicate with persons.

By default, change pins and password and enable MFA for all your account. Use a password manager which will give you the confidence to create and use more complex and difficult passwords to guess. Change you bank card and control its use.

Do allow default payment on online accounts to be created for your bank card and where they exist remove them from internet accounts. This means that you must process each payment were required and single click payment processing without any user verification is not enabled for any of your internet accounts.

Always ask the retailer for physical receipts, that is till receipts and bank card receipts that are sometime incorporated into the one receipt, for each transaction that you use your card for. It is a possibility this type of person is monitoring your home or workplace and as such if you feel this is the case, you should inform your employer if you have definite and overriding proof of this.

This will also entail informing police of this activity. Note that this type of stalking for financial gain is unfortunately commonplace in our society and should never be of the thought that you are being paranoid or on edge due to other related factors. Caution is always a recommended step.

We will be focusing on cashless payment on how many societies are moving completely towards a cashless society and thus increase use of card payments. Using a credit or debit card for payment is in essence a payment extension of your bank account current account. Instead of using an account number and sort code you are using a set of unique number generate on behalf of a credit card processing company such as Visa or MasterCard in which your bank associates with your specific bank account number.

When you initiate a card payment, the epos will access the credit card payment network and send a message to your bank verifying that the transaction amount can be covered by funds available in your account. The information to verify that you are the verified owner of the card, that is the pin of the card is hosted in the cards chip and does not need to dial up your banks servers to verify the card pin, hence the term chip and pin.

If you use tap and go then, this verification process is skipped, and the only part of the process is to verify that the correct funds are available in requested bank account. As a result, there is very little layers of security processing in any card payment. If you lose your card or its stolen and you don't notice because you have your card details save to apple pay or google pay, then someone could be using your card for an indefinite period without you noticing it.

The move towards people storing all their personal information on their mobile phone needs to be slowed down as the ramification for an individual, if they lose their phone but instead loses associated information such as parallel payment platform using the same bank accounts, mobile phones or passport details is a real danger.

Storing your loyalty cards, bank cards, travel card, password details and associated application on your mobile phone is a big convergence of data for any individual. The ability to find my device, remote swipe of device and restore data information to a new mobile phone user information does not remove the risk of a user's accounts being compromised but instead is a convenience of conscience as individuals are led to believe that employing these mobile phone services will negate the effect of their device becoming lost or stolen.

Tap and go requires, three consecutive transactions before a user will be prompted to enter in their pin for the next bank card transaction. This means at least three transactions of 50 euro or pounds could exist before the cards fail safe system kicks in. This is a maximum of 150 euro or pounds. This may seem like not much, but this encourages financial scammer to keep going knowing that there is a guaranteed maximum 150 euro or pound potentially available in every wallet or handbag.

This is worse than having cash on display as if a pin can be correctly guessed, transaction of greater amounts can be processed. The only recourse is using in shop CCTV images and match transaction time to epos and person processing transaction. After that the person would need to be tracked down. Most times these individuals are wearing methods of disguise such as baseball hats, dark glasses, or oversized clothes as they are knowing committing a financial crime.

The additional security measure by using bank cards as a form of photographic identity with an image of the card owner on the card was declined by credit card companies due to aesthetic reasons and rebranding or own branding of credit cards. Own branding is a credit card is branded to a specific company colours and logo. The dropping of this security measure is short sighed and lacks any adequate explanation. Other security mechanism such as maximum three tap were only recently introduced when it was realised that a person can still spend a lot of money using a maximum tap and go amounts of 50 euro or pounds per transaction.

The biggest existing threat is at the electronic points of sale, called epos. The standard bank issue epos evolved to included mobile app using a mobile phones NFC chip, generic epos or epos which come with their own questions in relation to firmware update of the epos hardware, and home brew solution which have been cobbled together from multiple differing technologies. With this type of epos, it has been easy to configure epos to clone bank cards.

All you need to do to clone a bank card is a hard drive or memory chip on the epos which instead of temporarily storing bank card information for verification purposes, stores the card details to be later used to burn on a generic bank card with no branding. If the cards details are to be used for online transactions only, the cv2 number will also be written down as this number is not stored on the card and then the bank card details are saved to a web browser form fill function and used when required.

The simplicity of cloning cards is frightful but there are some basic steps that you can take to prevent bank cards from be cloned.

Firstly, never let your card leave your hand. Always process the transaction, be it using pin or tap, should and can only legally be processed by the card owner.

Secondly always cover the terminal when entering your pin. This will prevent anybody been able using your card for transactions over 50 euro or pounds.

Thirdly, make sure that your wallet can block RFID signals so you card cannot be intentional scanned by an epos terminal without your consent.

Fourthly, do not store your bank card details on your mobile phone using either Apple Pay, Apple wallet, Google Pay or Pay Pal and equivalent applications. A physical card is much easier to control than a digital version of your bank card on your mobile phone.

Fifthly, if you are storing your bank card on your mobile phone ensure that you have a screen lock pin and fingerprint and facial recognition for access and identity control on your phone.

Sixthly, ensure you do not share bank card details with anybody, that is the only way your card details can be used is the physical use of your bank card for in shop purchases and the use of CV2 number for online purchases.

It makes sense for individuals to maintain or prune their current account in that their savings and investment are separate from their current account and thus as an individual to access your savings or investments, multiple level of security would be required.

Therefore, a sort of one-way traffic system would exist from a person's current account into their savings account and to unlock their savings account this could not easily done or be accessible. Online banking allows money transfer to occur global at the click of a mouse. This does open the possibility that current account could be used as a mechanism of money laundering. All international transaction of greater than 5000 euro or pounds are flagged by financial regulator authorities in most jurisdictions. As a result, you should never allow any other person access to your online banking account.

All direct debits or standing order emanating from your account should be initiated by yourself. If this is not the case, immediately cancel direct debits and reinstate were necessary required direct debits. Direct debit mandates must always be cancelled by both parties, by yourself at your bank and by who the direct debit is intended for. If this is not the case, direct debits may continue to be legally processed even if you have cancelled the direct debit mandate.

It may be the case that the service provider tries to slow the process down if you cancel an internet service and associated direct debit for payment. If you feel this is the case, consult the authorities around cancellation of services outside a fixed term contract and know what your rights are. If you need to seek redress for services cancel for which you are still paying for, then either change your bank account details or inform you bank that you have cancelled this direct debit, informed the service provider in question and as far you are concern have follow the correct legal avenue and thus this type of transaction can only be illegal but fraudulent. As a result, the bank is legal obliged to inform the relevant internal department of such activities and investigate were necessary.

Internet protocol range addresses has expanded from version IP Version 4 addressing system to IP Version 6 addressing system. What this means is large amount or addresses can be directed access without the need to go through a firewall or internet routing. The amount of directly addressable devices from the internet has greatly increased.

So, we have cut out the middleman and know when we call a server for a request it is directly routed to that server and not through any network address translation protocol. What these means is that the addresses that access these servers is only known by the server who has accessed the server and not by any other network device. So instead of ISP's accumulation information on who is accessing what, now it is the owner of these publicly facing servers. The ramification of this shift has yet to be fully realised but as you can see less moving part means less transparency and less transparent is the enemy of democracy. As there are multiple ways you can connect to an internet facing server either through copper cables, fibre cables, 5G cell tower network or through a satellite internet connection the route to the data source is irrelevant and meaningless to most parties, however from a server point of view you can exactly see who is accessing what, when, from where and for how long.

This information from an advertisement point of view is gold and does not need to be scraped from a person internet cookie, web browser activity, internet connection provider or their internet accounts. This information is contiguous, full, real, true, verified, accurate, up to date and most importantly monetizable. So therefore, the data holders of the future will not be governments, ISP's, server farms or those agencies instructed for data protection, but the individual owners of websites hosted on servers in a data centre.

Just like a wiretap in the old days, distributed systems have pushed intelligent data down the data line to the individual. Therefore, just like influencers and bloggers they will be the person who generate the next generation of internet products and services and not the current large internet companies. This may go counter to popular belief and dystopian views of the world but that is where technology is leading to.

Just like the present-day utility companies of water, electricity, and gas. They will not push Internet growth forward but simple be resource providers and resources as an enabler not a doer. So as the large internet and media companies reach their crescendo and fall back to their state as incumbent utility companies, fresh faces and ideas will come to the fore.

Internet security will be the responsibility of everyone, that is why identity theft is such an important topic now as an individual's identity is a driver of growth either as a consumer or as a provider.

So, before we get to that concept of future internet growth, we need to deal with the present realities of internet use and how we can prevent our identity from be used by other person or worse still aspects of our lives being used by other individuals. I have covered from a technical point of view what we can do but now we will look at from a non-technical point that is human skills and modern-day con artists who have embraced the internet age and spread their skills and knowledge. The first point that I must make is to do with secrecy and confidentiality. This I feel is a human skill that has been watered down increasingly over time. The basic and embarrassing reason for this is people associate gossip with popularity. Juicy gossip as it is called because everybody loves a bit of gossip now and then.

A person spreading gossip, or worse still false truths and accuracy has been seen as the arena of the media however these types of rumours either start at the school gates, at coffee shops or at workplace socials to name just a few. This is where we sort of let our guard down and to access the cliché of a workplace or social place, we may start off with idle small talk and gossip.

This kind of activity can spiral into something that it was not intent to be but alas the damage is done. There is no way to roll back what has happened now and what has been said. As such this information once presented in a digital form will take on a whole new life and live in the perennials that is the internet.

Data harvesters, whose job is to build up a digital picture of an individual for monetizing purposed will exploit this to their benefit. As such certain items about an individual life and personality could be inserted to the digital profile unbeknownst to them.

This occurs during various background checks and vetting process for data sensitive jobs in our society. What may have been generate as gossip and ideal truth may be converted from gossip to truth when it comes to these types of checks because he said, and she said so.

Where we draw the line between fact and fiction is at most times difficult to Gauge and this is why we have a courts system for such reason, but unfortunately very few times is the court system relied upon for such instances as the truth about someone's background which when goes uncheck has very damaging and long-term impacts for an individual.

So, prevention is better than cure, if you do not know something to be verifiably true, it is your right as an individual and citizens of society not to spread false and idle gossip because the loop can be small, and these situations can come back to haunt us.

Traveling and cyber security. When travelling it is best to register with your foreign affairs department your travel itinerary before you leave. Also travel insurance should cover any digital devices you are travelling with. Many people assume that home insurance covers digital devices when travelling. This is not the case as your home insurance policy is based on contents in situ and not when taken outside the home or abroad. As such if dependent upon your digital devices for flight tickets, train tickets, hotel booking confirmation and satnav maps for navigating your way a new city or location, then if they become loss or stolen, this could greatly affect your travel plans and your visit.

Always ensure that you have your digital devices content backed up to the cloud either as a complete rebuild; this is where if you lose your device, you purchase a similar or same device and use the restore from backup when configuring the replacement device for the first time. Alternatively, you can back up individual applications data to the cloud which is independent of what mobile device operating system is that you are using. The alternative is to backup individual travel plans as individual files such as pdf's and then save these files to a cloud storage location such as Microsoft One Drive, Google G drive or Drop Box.

A little bit of planning can go a long way and take care when using your digital device in public abroad, especially when navigating a new location, as you will be easily spotted and could become an easy target. Some ways to avoid becoming a target is always get a cover for your digital device as it makes it difficult for others to identity what kind of device you are using. Some professional thieves will only target certain devices where the registered device can be unlocked from the operating system and thus wipe and rebuilt to be sold on.

Thieves these days on will steel what can be easily sold on as such web sites as eBay and Amazon. The quality of second-hand devices is high in the resale marketplace as people who want to reduce their carbon footprint will intentionally buy refurbished devices. This means that second hand stolen devices have a limited if not niche devices. As such it may be the case that if your device is stolen and the thief is unable to crack the operating system password before being remotely locked and wiped then the devices may simply be switched off and dumped as there is no further use that can be gained from them.

Another cause for concern is the method off payments that you use. If you are using Apple Pay or Google Pay, remember these methods are tied to your bank card associated with your bank account. It is prudent to inform your bank before you leave the country, as bank systems use artificial intelligence algorithms and trained person to look for anomalous spending patterns with their customers. If for some reason the bank systems highlight a customer who is using their bank card in many different jurisdictions at the same time, they may freeze your bank card until further investigations are carried out.

This may require you to reverify your details with your bank. If abroad this extra hassle that you do not need and may cause additional complications. So even though the internet has opened a lot of borders for us and made travel and spending easier, all original concern to do with bank accounts and financial transactions still exist. So always pay the same amount of attention when your card is being processed for a transaction.

Travelling is a seen as common place these days whether for work or for pleasure. There are some concerns you should address before travelling for work purposes. Remember when working in any location you and your contents, including your digital devices, are covered by your work insurance policy as opposed to any other insurance policy that you may have. If you need to claim against an insurance policy and you are working on official business, then you must claim from your work insurance policy as other insurance policies that you may have may be void because of being on official work-related business.

Make a note of all your digital devices both work related and personal and if using personal devices for work related business or your workplace has a Bring Your Own Device policy in place you need to define who takes responsibility for what in the event of lost or theft. Nowadays most places using bring your own device policy will ask the employees to take full responsibility for the device both and associated ICT technical support, provisioning the device that matches the organisations recommended guidelines and insuring devices against loss or theft.

Ensure that you have adequate back up of data and devices if devices become damaged, lost, or stolen. The best form of back up, that is operating system independent is the back up of application data to the cloud. Also ensure that you have a password manager for your work-related password as a separate vault password to that of your personal passwords.

Never mix your personal applications with work applications even if there is cross over of applications as in the creative sphere, it may be difficult to delineate between personal and work-related content especially if you are sub-contracting your services to other organisations.

When travelling ensure you have cash in the local currency. In countries that are fully cashless ensure you bring another form of payment such as a credit and debit card, but a non-electronic form of payment accepted in the region that you are travelling in is highly recommended. If possible, pay for everything in advanced of departing. Also, if holidaying you could avail of all-inclusive resort cutting down on the need for methods of payments.

If creating on an account with an online bank, ensure that it is incorporated in the jurisdiction that you live in especially if it is a new bank not connected to an incumbent bank within your country. Internet bank can pop up and extensively advertise to build up a large customer base with little deposits from this customer base or backing the banking entity itself. This internet bank could easily fold or merge with other banking entities if they are incorporate in a different jurisdiction.

The 2008 financial crisis turned a lot of people off the traditional way of banking and the main banks within a country. As a result, such financial products as crypto currencies have seen unprecedented growth due to public demand to have a decentralised currency and currency exchange. Prices for goods and services are dictated by the simple supply and demand curve for the currency and not government policy or currency manipulation of currency monopolisation.

As internet banks have been able to setup relatively easily as they do not have a high street presence and are making use of established technologies in the form of online banking which is accepted by the public as the way day to day banking will evolve. This acceptance of technology, business practices and public demand has led people to use internet banks to safeguard their current and savings accounts then they would have done twenty or thirty years ago.

Banking then was seen as needing to have big offices, fat profit margins and a status quo approach to business. As a result, ICT security in the financial sector has grown more than in any other sector of an economy. That means more cyber-attacks are focus on the financial sector than in any other sector. As the population has incremental increased through the decades without a population explosion, this means technology is being used to fight technology, that is large bot nets are specifically being focused on financial institutes to compromise and access their networks and customer accounts.

As this is a costly approach, these types of cyber attackers will focus on countries in the world with a high yearly gross domestic product. So, this logic draws us to the conclusion that northern hemisphere countries are under the greatest combined threat from cyber hackers. So, this means that cybers hackers are actively working within the countries of where the most cyber hacks are occurring or very close to them.

This also means that they must have some inside knowledge of the ICT architecture of the banks they are trying to hack. They may build up this picture by befriending employees of a bank or monitor their activities to use their access and login credentials for their place of work. This is a scary picture being painted but it is quite factually true. The monitoring of employees of a particular organisation to use their access code or keys to get into a organisations ICT network is not new but has come from monitoring government departments and agencies employees for nefarious reasons, to other parts of the economy such as the private sector.

People in areas of responsibilities within such organisations do receive training on spotting and reporting such activities however it is easier than ever to monitor a person's activities remotely either through the placing of monitoring equipment within a person's home residence, using existing CCTV networks such as in shopping centres or public spaces and monitoring an individual's activity so as not to make the person aware.

Also it is the case that people monitoring or following you will make you aware of what they are doing either to panic you and make you make a mistake or reveal something that you did not intend to do but in general this practise is seen as shaking the tree to see what comes out and it is a sign that the person monitoring you have run out of option and information as has not garnered any new or useful information to use against you. They will mostly likely move on in a few days. From CCTV images, we can gather such information as where a person works, lives, socialises, and holidays and at such a point they will use such techniques as social engineering to expand upon the information already gathered. This information is then used in the process of cyber hacking and attacking and organisations ICT infrastructure for personal gain.

Chapter 9 – Work/Life Balance

We have already looked at the technical aspects with working from different locations other than your workplace office. Here, we will look at method to disconnect from your work and ways to achieve a more balanced life.

Always on, always available, that is what the internet is, and we are no longer confined to working or living the usually dawn to dusk hours. As a result, a lot of people are over stimulated between increased coffee drink, device usage and more active and busy life. This has left people very little time to disconnect, unwind and to leave it at the office.

People are seeking solace in such activities a yoga, go to the gym or other outdoor activity.

However, just like implementing screen time restrictions on their phone and device usage, this is something adults need to also view and look at themselves. Right to disconnect for work reason will only create the legal framework for people to apply their own disconnect from technology mechanisms.

If devices are available and work needs to be done, persons maybe implored to work regardless of the circumstances. What the solution is being offered is digital detox. Just like any addiction a person will go cold turkey with no access to digital device, normally accommodated in group accommodations with other similar person in similar circumstances. People receive group and individual treatments. The person seeking this kind of support are workaholics and online gamers who play and work, day, and night with no ability to disconnect.

The ways that you can disconnect are firstly, if do not have to hybrid work then base yourself in your work office. This is a physical and metal barrier between your work and personal life.

Secondly, leave all work devices and correspondence at the office.

Thirdly, make it clear to fellow workers that all work matters must be addressed in the workplace and do not give out your personal mobile number out to work colleagues. HR departments normal have a person's personal mobile number, so instruct them not to give out your personal number to anybody.

Fourthly, Planning. If you properly plan your workday then hidden surprise should not develop, somebody's else's crisis is not your crisis, and it is up to everyone to act in professional manner. Do not be bated into working in an environment that is constantly firefighting issues with little or no planning, direction, or management. This is not how workplaces are supposed to work.

Fifthly, if you do need to carry a work device then don't carry one otherwise have defined on/off or availability times stated in all outgoing communications. Have a justified reason for carrying a work device. Having a work phone is no longer seen as a perk of any job. Sixthly, state in work email your office hours and hours availability. Anything that falls outside that will the responded upon only during those hours.

Employers are now rolling back hybrid working availability and hours to persons they managed. That is hybrid working is being limited to certain days of the week and to certain individuals. The reason for this is that some employees were working more than one job at a time this included rearing their family during work hours (school runs, family meals and babysitting for others) when they should of being using their maternity or paternity leave instead. As a result, these employees were less easy to manage while working at home or in a remote hub.

Bosses are returning to a structured workday with defined work hours and delegation of duties. It is unfortunate that hybrid working has led to these abuses of trust and responsibilities and now bosses are requiring their staff to have a business case for remotely working. As a result, hybrid working trial by fire because of COVID-19 has raised certain questions, restrictions and best practises that need to be implemented.

Diet is an important aspect to a healthy work/life balance. A person who's work inconstantly in crisis, always travelling between meeting and meeting or travelling international living put of a suitcase and out of restaurants is going to unfortunately lead an unhealthy life either eating too much or too little were achieving their ideal weight is going to become a constant battle.

The only true way to lead a healthy and fulfilling life is to have some aspect of your life and lifestyle that is non-negotiable with your boss. A clear life that no one should cross and if your boss or work colleagues do cross then it's time to look around for a new job. This Rubicon or line in the sand is your fixed point in your life from which you can branch out and structure your life.

For most people, this is their children or family life. That is their welfare and safety come before anything else and your boss and fellow employees should beware of this. If it is a case between what takes preference in a work situation, finish a work project of you family life, your family life will take preference.

From this fixed point you can structure and prioritise other aspects of your life. The best form of diet is not calorie counting or running to the gym everyday but instead is buying a weekly shopping that is planned out and learning to cook for yourself. Not only will you eventually start to cook more and more healthier dishes, but you will also expand your palate and understanding of different cuisine.

Knowing where the best restaurants are in a city is not the same as being able to cook the dishes that they serve. Learn the basics of cooking and the rest will follow. You'll not only save a lot of money, but you will also start to look and act a lot healthier.

Setting limits for things that you do is also important. Do not get consumed by any one habit or way of doing something. Variety is the spice of life, so try do things in a different way or something different altogether. The internet has expanded are abilities to try new things, so do not be a fool not to embrace this resource waiting at our fingertips.

The internet is not just for work and internet shopping but is a lot more cultured than some cities that we inhabit.

It is not balance in moderation, which is a boring approach to do something, but find out what your own likes and dislikes are as opposed to someone else likes and dislikes are which we have inherited by spending too much time in one place or with one group of people. Life is there to be enjoyed not endured so the internet is your friend not your enemy, as seeing it as a battle of internet speeds, times or other resources is not a healthy thought or approach.

Life without the internet. The internet is not old enough for us to imagine what life would be like without the internet. Its creation has been a slow linear curve from the days man first try to communicate with its neighbours for such things as warning of impending attacks to celebrations using fire and smoke such as lighthouse, of fires on the top of hills or mountains. Communication has been about intent with acknowledgment or receipt of message to intended party required. So, the internet is the digitisation of a process that has been occurring for many years and as such has easily become part of any society due to it underlining fundamentals being based on sound human logic and principles.

How the internet will change human behaviour and how human interact is the more important question. No doubt it has led to efficiencies, greater choice, and options and free to work and play. However, these advances or changes in our behaviour and led us to lead busier as opposed to more fulfilling lives. The constant need to check devices for stimulus is a worrying trend and akin to lighting up a cigarette. As fingers and minds are easily bored and the ability to switch off complete and drop what we are doing is becoming more and more difficult to do for the average individual.

Chapter 10 – Internet for Children and Online Bullying

Children and the internet. There are many internet products available to parents that police your child's internet activity without you having to look over their shoulders. These products are either incorporated into the operating system of the device such as apple screentime, family share, Microsoft internet security products or Google android security settings for profiles.

However as good as these products are and with the best intentions in mind, this does not stop your child buying a burner mobile phone, which is a phone which is untraceable, originally only available on the dark web, and using this device to hide their internet activity. These burner phones are available to anybody, and you do not need to eighteen to own one.

A child can carry out all their nefarious activities that they want to hide from their parents and at the first sign things may be getting hot, chuck the phone and cool off and then get a new burner phone. There is nothing to stop any parent from preventing their child from behaving in this manner, short of searching them when they enter their home.

It is always parents' way to see their children in the best possible light as they see them as extensions of themselves however a dose of reality is as much required for parents about the goings on of the internet in the twenty first century as it is for their children.

This book will shed some light on these goings on but as a parent you must use you best judgement to identify these activities and challenge you child in a non-offensive and non-confrontational way if you feel something is going on and going wrong.

As most activities require money, giving you child weekly pocket money and ways to earn extra pocket money is one to divert their time and attention away from dangerous activities.

Using family functions and setting them up with a Revolute account or other online bank account is a way to give them the freedom they need as growing individuals to explore their individuality but at the same time as a parent be able to manage and not control their activities. This way they can know the value of money and what is takes to earn money at a young enough age which will stand to them down the line when looking to branch out on their own.

These online accounts can be an extension of your own account, a child account, or an online account for a child.

The best approach is a child account associated with your own bank account where monies can be easily transferred without any additional bank cost. A weekly minimum pocket money with a maximum top limit should be agreed with your child.

All spending by your child can be monitored by yourself or even approved by yourself before purchase. A child will be learning how to spend appropriately, avoiding impulse buying, how to save their money for a big purchase, how to keep an eye on their money, the need to review their monthly bank statements and how to read a bank statement properly, and overall money management techniques.

This single approach could be the best way to avoid your child running into difficulties.

The next worry is online bullying and your child. These days, bully is not only in the school yard and outside the school gates but has now evolved online and has created its presence online manifesting as new forms of bullying that did not appear before.

The internet has created group bullying technique. This is where individuals band together to take down an individual and try to affect their mental health and break their spirit.

This is not a punch or elbow to the face but something far worse that children are ill equipped to the deal with at such a young age. You probably have seen it as Facebook post but because you not on the inside and are unaware at what to look out for; but such group post is meant not to just offend or hurt an individual but really to cause long term damage to an individual personality, character and their make up as a human being.

Schools and parents are aware of such activities but really, they are only catching the tip of the iceberg as just as when you were at school ratting on you school peer will cause you to become unpopular and hated by classmates and school mates.

So, the best thing for a child who is being bullied is that an adult sees what's going on an act upon it. That is, they report is to the school, police or social service and waits to ensure that the information has been acted on. It is best in these circumstances not to act as some sort of vigilante and try to take the issue on yourself.

Children are not stupid, and they know very well, being children how to play dumb or innocent and conceal what is really going on. To report such activity, you really do need hard proof. Hearsay is the enemy of justice and just like any potential legal case, proof is required before an investigation can begin.

If you do see messages, you can report this content as harmful to the internet service provider such as Facebook. But as Facebooks subscribers are in the billions; no doubt Facebook is using some artificial intelligence bot to do the grunt work and human eyes will only screen content further down the line.

What you are looking for is sustained verbal attacks against one specific individual or internet account. These posts or text message should be documented in chronological order. As bully's send or post message the veracity of the message will become worse and worse.

If this is the case, then psychology 101 would say that the bully is mentally unstable and a person that authorities and social service should take a closer look. Obliviously, we need to know that the actual account used to post the messages is indeed tied to the individual in questions and not somebody else masquerading as another individual in question which does happen.

How we can verify that this is the person who is the bully is either through their email address, the location that the account is originating from, or other picture and post that will tie them to a social event, calendar appointment or verification by one of their close family members.

You must remember you can only go so far to prove or disprove the existence of an online bully. If it is something not easily proved, then only take it to a predefined point. Bully's like to live in the open and in the public eye and are looking for attention, to be noticed, to become popular amongst their peers or to come across as hard if they are trying to join a gang.

All these reasons need public acknowledgment so gathering proof if an individual is a bully should be straight forward. A bully who lives in the shadow maybe down the line bordering on becoming a murderer or serial killer however this is a big jump but still warrants being noted.

So, the forms of online bullying will either be text based, Facebook posts, mobile text messages, video based, Tik Tok videos, fans only videos, audio only content which can use any number of internet platforms, encrypted sites such as what's App or visual based using photos which again can use any number of internet platforms.

It is the case with internet platform to screen content before uploaded and have users 'sign' terms and conditions of use before using an internet service. However, there are always ways around this, and such ways is to upload content that is only offensive to the individual or embarrassing to the individual being bullied.

Next is to upload content that has been modified in some way to fool artificial intelligence screening software. This can consist of obscuring content in such a way that makes it difficult to read by software such as ordering pixels in a way that becomes reordered once passed through artificial intelligence software.

Other ways are to splice and upload images separately and once uploaded on a platform join on a single post. Not all internet content platforms screen content before upload and it is the case in copyrights infringement that lawyers will contact internet service provider with cease-and-desist order to take down content, or for legal authorities the removal of harmful content.

Educating our children to the hidden dangers of internet use and just like being taught about stranger danger in public this should also be extended to internet safe use. You should have a kill switch on your internet connection, that is the ability to take your home network offline at the switch off a button.

If not, using you home network for such use as home security or a doorbell, you can use your routers power button as a kill switch. Other methods of internet kill swich could be disabling your home Wireless LAN, which most devices use to connect to your home router. Only wired devices would work. Other kill switch would be changing the subnet mask of your home address to a Class B address which would not allow any devices to connect to your home router.

As mentioned, it is easy for internet application to be used for purposes other than their intended purpose and this is the case with cyber bullying.

Cyber bullying does and can happen on all the major social media platforms and messaging services, but it seems that WhatsApp has become a personal favourite with cyber bullies. The reason may be that bullies can public shame or hurt individuals in plain view of other persons using WhatsApp groups. WhatsApp uses encryption to encrypt messages between client applications. As a result, messages and content is not monitored in real time like that is done by Meta's applications of Facebook and Instagram.

As a result, it is easy for online bullying to grow unchecked and unmonitored out of the gaze of authorities and adults. As such WhatsApp groups can become grooming rooms using to spread misinformation, hate material and other content not beneficial to society.

As a result, WhatsApp groups can be hijacked for other reason than their intended reason. If you are parent of a young adult, you should regular check your child's device for content and messaging threads containing such content. Using firewalls and content blockers on your home network only goes so far and applying a multi-layer approach to IT security for your family is not a practical approach when trying to address online bullying concerns.

The best approach is content filtering at the internet connection level and not device level as there are many ways to circumnavigating these security aspects, one being than your child knows your home security password for the internet router. You should disable Wi-Fi networking on the device, that is not allow the device to connect to any Wi-Fi network be it your home network or public available Wi-Fi network. As a result, the only internet connection available for your child to use is your mobile operator's data plan and 5G network.

Next cap the data plan that you have with your mobile provider to a fixed monthly amount. Most mobile operator use a fair usage policy for their data plans, but you can still implement a fixed monthly data allowance or bundle with a mobile operator.

Next ensure that your data plan with your mobile provider has a content filter functionality associated with it. That is any data connection will be filtered for profanities, offensive material, and content not appropriate for a person of that age group.

Now you are not responsible for content filtering, and you have outsourced the problem to a professional internet service provider. Your children now cannot circumnavigate your home networking internet connection for nefarious reasons.

Chapter 11 – Social Networks

Social networks are embedded into online gaming platforms and gaming consoles. Gaming consoles have now really evolved into online gaming communities using a power chip processor to access internet content. Gaming consoles have powerful processor that are required for graphic processing and games speed. Many fail safes exist to ensure age-appropriate content is only available and accessible to person whose age has been verified. This age verification process is also tied to method of purchase of content from the game's consoles online store.

However, it is the responsibility of parents to ensure that content being used on these games console is age appropriate for the supposed audience. If still a minor, a young adult will still require parents or guardians' consent for the setup of online gaming account and a method of purchase.

Gaming friends and communities are moderated by online gaming communities' moderators and were requested gamers who infringed upon agreed gaming communities' terms and conditions of account may have their account frozen or removed from a gaming communities' platform.

Content is moderated for bad language, expletives, offensive material, or inappropriate behaviour to fellow gamers. As such the main gaming network that are used are safe to persons of all ages. However, a word of caution is required. Some of these gaming consoles have been jail break, this means that they can behave in a manner that the designer of the game's consoles did not intend them to operate as. This can include by passing safety protocols and circumnavigating security systems intended to prevent gaming platform being used for nefarious reason.

Some of these including an extension to the dark web were a host of illegal goods and services can be purchased.

Some games consoles have been networked together to perform such tasks as testing the impact of a nuclear warhead on a city, nuclear fallout map and processing other types of data that requires high performing processor to perform such calculations. As such that power of these processors should not be underestimated.

There are social media sites for friends and family and there are social media sites for professions, employment, and organisation in the workspace. People are under the assumption that what do not put on their professional site is ok to put on your social media site, so if it's not ok for LinkedIn then its ok for Facebook. This is not something that does not rings true.

First, if you are going for most jobs these jobs, some form of background check occurs. The level and detail of these background check varies but any basic background check will look at your internet presence and profile.

Therefore, before you post, comment or like any content on any public viewable and accessible site always ensure that the content matches the audience. If any doubt or deviation occurs, then be safe and don't post, comment or like.

The main reason for this is what is posted, commented, or liked on the internet can stay up there for a very long time and trying to get anything removed from public viewable can take time and resources. Also remember to check you profile settings to see how much content of your profile is viewable and for how far reaching the content is.

Remember that your public profile settings can be different to another person's so they may share on content not originally intended for a specific audience. This is the case for differing social media sites and channel who use different terminologies and approaches to the sharing of content and implementing privacy policies and interpretation of legislation with the intent of implementing features for their user's accounts.

So, where you may have intended a comment, post or like to be viewable to a select view, this maybe circumnavigated and be shared on to a larger or different audience. This can have unattended consequences.

Some social media sites like snapchat, content is only available for a short period of time and then disappear. Persons like this way of real time content that is only available, viewable, and relevant for a very short period. After that the content disappears.

This is avoiding content overload as content is time stamped for a specific set period. However, this functionality does not extend to a lot of other social media sites as content is monetizes through clicks, like and shares so the longer content is around, the more likely content will increase its monetisation ability.

Your internet account setting for a social media account can run a security check and show which and what content from your profile is viewable. Remember that additional features and functions are added to these platforms, so it is important to check and view to see that your privacy settings are still relevant. Settings and layout greatly differ from one platform to another, and so does terminology so make sure you understand phrases and words used and associated function. Always included a profile pic on your social media profile to avoid anyone else trying to use your name or character for their own purposes. Make this publicly viewable as this will discourage anybody else from using your digital profile.

Food delivery services. The explosion of food delivery services during covid-19 has led to consolidation within the industry as food delivery platform consolidate to bring delivery costs down, and merge technologies. Normally food deliver companies are using the same application and technology across the industry with some food delivery companies' technology being hosted in the same data centre and servers and their largest competitor.

Thus, consolidation of competitors has only cost the merger in rebranding costs and everything else is the same in terms of technology and headcount. A such it is important as a consumer, when creating a new internet account that you keep track of accounts that you create for such purposes. Normally these types of accounts will allow you to save your personal details, payments process, previous orders, and favourite orders to your account. Very little security is available for these types of accounts, with most only needing a username and password to access your account.

It has been the case where people have accessed other persons food delivery services accounts and changed the delivery address to another address and ordered using the payment card given on the account. The person only finds out that this has happened if they review their bank statements or during the next order review previous order.

In the meantime, the delivery address will have been changed back to the original delivery address unbeknownst to the account holder.

Also, the mobile contact number may have been changed if delivery status updates are provided by text message.

This sneaky approach has no come back and usually the address provided for the fraudulent order is an apartment block with the incorrect apartment number where the perpetrator will normally meet the delivery driver at the main door. The delivery driver most likely will not be able to provide a photofit of the person as the person may have a disguise such as wearing a wig, baseball cap or fake beard.

The order will be substantial enough to warrant a person to instigate the process in the first place. This activity is not uncommon and can happen quietly and silently without being noticed.

The internet and legacy accounts. Recent legislation in various countries allows you as an individual to have published content on the internet be remove or taken down by request by request to the internet content provider directly.

This right to be forgotten process askes the various internet service providers such as Google to remove content that is directly about you from appearing in their search results and on hosted websites that they control.

This does go some way to removing content no longer relevant about a person or where some specific period has elapsed, and content is no longer of public interest.

However as always ensure that if you are requesting content to be taken down that it may respawn in a different guise on the internet for the fact that you requested its removal. Remember a lot of internet revenue is generate by clicks, like and shares so if someone believes that revenue can still be generated from this content then its requested removal could renew interest again in the content.

This is just human nature and should not frustrate attempts for removal of published internet content.

In most internet accounts and social media accounts there is the function of legacy accounts. That is where an account becomes inactive or an individual passes on, there is a process as to what happens to the internet account and associated content.

You can set functionality and features in your social media sites, that if there is no new activity on the account for a specific set period of time and after a set number of warnings to the holder of the accounts, if not reactivated or someone does not log into the account, all content of the account and associated with the account on a specific internet service provider servers will be deleted.

The alternative is to name a next of kin as your contact on the internet service provider account and they will be able to access the account and make some amendments and changes and make the account legacy account in your memory. No new content would be able to be generated for the account and the account would be a sort of in a suspended animation, but a person's account would live on, on the internet.

Alternatively, your next of kin can keep your account in legacy for a period before closing it down entirely. These are settings that you can decide upon yourself. Obviously, it is important to whom you choose as your next of kin as they may use this as a back door to access your internet accounts.

If in doubt, use the delete function after set period as your default option, and review this setup when you feel the need for this option arises.

Chapter 12 – Job Hunting with the Internet

Job searching and the internet. The internet is a very useful resource when searching for a job. You can get tips and templates for you cv, search for available jobs, prepare for you interview by reaching organisation, how to get to the interview and how to prepare questions and answers for the interview.

Therefore, people spend a considerable amount of time searching for a new job. However, to get noticed and attract potential employers to our CV or internet profile we tend to put more information in our CV's or internet profile than is necessary or relevant for most roles and jobs.

That is, we create a master template of all our social, employment and educational information and from that we create bespoke CV's, job applications and online profiles for such an intended purpose. And as we are all too aware of, data harvester intentional search the internet for these kinds of information, as in some way job searching is seen as a vulnerability or weakness in a person's current situation, one which can easily be exploited by persons with nefarious intentions.

Ensure any entities that you share information about your job status have a written contract with, and you are not simply uploading you CV on mass to the internet hopping to get lucky that an employer will think you are the right person for the job. With any job there are many screening out processes that will whittle any potential candidate down to a few individuals for a face-to-face interview. This is the standard process and no other way to legal obtain a job within an economy. All jobs must be advertised to the public to be considered a role or job in an organisation, even if these roles are unpaid, interns or volunteers' positions.

We may tend to give out more information or over-elaborate where necessary. It is certainly the environment where employment agencies or potential employers advertise non-existent roles in an organisation to increase public profile, giving their HR department something to do and a cheap way to provided training to their staff.

Other reason could be more hidden, such as seeing what the competition is at by creating job descriptions that attract a certain calibre of candidate, and when this person is at an interview, they are asked probing questions about up-and-coming research and development products or marketing campaigns.

Other reason could be to poach potential employees from a competitor or get an update on employees within a different organisation. The reason can be many and as such we should never send our CV out on mass to jobs that are available but research each job advertisement, getting the job description and role pack that is normally available for each advertised job and only after carefully reviewing the job, should we then decide whether the role is for us or not to explore further.

HR department have in the past used outsource employment agencies to do the initial leg work, screening out candidates and conducting initial interviews and skills assessment before selecting candidates for an organisations final round interview.

Yet these outsourced employment agencies will have their own modus operand and may only move forward candidates that they feel may give them further insight into an organization or they may only advertise or inform individuals about a role who are aligned with a particular employment agency.

This practise is more common than you think, and the internet has created a cassum between employers and potential employees with employment agencies being the gate keepers allowing only people with their preferences to progress to a potential job and employer.

So, to protect or online profile and career profile, we should be very selected in the career information that we put in our cv or on our professional career web sites.

Also, it has been the case where persons who never worked for an organisation, add content to their CV based on second hand information about projects they worked on or management structure and reporting structures within an organisation.

When it comes to references and backing up this information, they may have a friend in an organisation who's number they give out to act as a fake reference for the time they supposedly worked in an organisation. They may present credential such as business card, contact details including genuine email address and contact numbers, a LinkedIn profile verified as an employee of the organisation, organisation stationery and marketing products such as bags with company logo on them.

They may say something like they prefer to give their reference in person as to over the phone because they feel this is a safer and more secured and verified form of giving a reference when they are laying the groundwork to confirm in an employer's mindset the Genuity of their reference.

All this can be created by internet companies for this specific function without the requirement to verify that you do indeed work for the organisation in question. This reference can be bought as a service and be paid for using crypto currency which is untraceable.

Meanwhile an organisation has hired an employee which does not have the required skillset for the job. As a result, this fake candidate employee, will have a 'go forth and multiply approach' and will try to hire persons of a similar ilk to themselves to hide their own secret so that if it does come out about their identity, then other persons are there to take the fall.

This has a very destructive influence on an organisation and without definitive proof could be responsible for financial crisis in the past, were no doubt about it, unskilled and untrained persons were certainly making some very serious decisions in the dark with little or no experience or understanding of the outcome.

A review of the financial crisis in the past shows that some players who rose up through the ranks did not have some basic training in emotional intelligence, over leveraging, daily limits, or proper reporting structure for both internal and external reporting of financial anomalies.

As a result of this lack of oversight on the persons employed at an organisation by either internal HR department or outsourced recruiters responsible for head hunting individuals otherwise known as poaching, has led to serious repercussions for the banking sector in the last two decades.

As we have seen, this type of activity has led to the public looking for a decentralized form of currency such as cryptocurrencies currently in circulation.

Also, less complex financial and investment products where actual gain is modest but guaranteed such as government bonds.

Also, the increase in online internet banks only existing on the internet which are easily to set up, control and close if required. Legislation on setting up bank accounts for money laundering purposes did little to stop the financial crisis of the past where the greatest influence lay within the buildings of the banks and not in the public.

So again, information is power and in the new information age, this has unintended and unforeseen consequences.

The only way to ensure that the employees' you employ are who they say they are and have experience in the required fields is either to employee straight out of university and put them on your own internal training and performance review process which is expensive and unless you have employee's loyalty from the outset, this will be the first type of employee poached by another organisations.

Secondly, candidates must sign a full disclosure agreement with the organisation, which disclosure for reasons of a full background check all information deemed relevant for the employment process. You will not always get the agreement of potential employees to this process, as it can be very intrusive, extensive and is a deep dive into somebody's existence for the purpose of getting a job which may be a bridge to far for most people.

The next alternative approach is to hire a person with a basic background check but for the initial probation period, they are assigned into a position directly below what they role advertised for. You would again need the employee's full cooperation for this, but if they have the necessary skillset, they should excel in the role and be brought up to the agreed position in no time at all.

However, if a performance review is required, then the employee did not possess all the stated skillset and they would either quit the role or remain in the roles in a reduced earning capacity.

Either way both employee and employer are in a learning capacity and this audit of skills in the workplace may be the only true way to measure a person performance which is not kin to learning on the job but doing on the job what you should know already.

This process would require the cooperation of the hiring manager, financial controller and HR department as some leeway would be required to facilitate an audit of a new hire's skillset. Obviously, it would be the intent that the new hire would be brought up to the agreed hired level based on fixed, impartial, and clearly defined explanation of skillsets displayed in the workplace.

This practise could be confused as a form of benchmarking or box ticking exercise, but it is anything but and it means that in the future, person is knowledgeable of the roles of people around them and not just the extent of their own roles, and thus can pitch in on new ideas and concepts if required.

HR department would need a fundamental review to stamp out such practises as unhelpful hiring practises which ultimately hinder the growth and development of an organisation. This means that each role in an organisation would need to be clearly defined, where the position sits within the organisation hierarchy, the position directly above and below advertised role and the limitation or definitions of these roles and the skillset that is required to successfully takeover or apply for these positions within an organisation.

This means that positions would be fixed, defined, and would leave very little wiggle room to hire person that are not an exact match for the role in the first place. This maybe too limiting for some organization who tend to see themselves in the internet age as fast moving and keeping up with the times to stay relevant and recent.

Chapter 13 – Data Breaches

Information is power and information's is powerful in the wrong hands. Do not underestimate the amount of data that we create daily, that is recorded and stored on the internet. Most of this data is legally obtained and has a technical requirement for collecting, such as meta data, however when unauthorised persons access this information this is where data breaches and information hacks become dangerous.

It is important as an individual to check all information that we save to the cloud or to internet services providers to see what information is stored on us. Most j have a Freedom of Information Act where we can request information being held about ourselves from any organisation or company. It is u to make use, where available, this piece of legislation, as it could affect our credit rating, police vetting or even community standings if information is held by an that is untrue or factually incorrect.

Data breaches are synonymous with the growth of the internet. There are websites that can be used to see if any online presence that you use have be compromised with your user information. If you are a heavy internet user, I would recommend a password manager, which also manages your online profile in real-time. If a website has been breached, your password manager will prompt you to change your password and show what disclosed information has been leaked in real time.

You should regular run an audit of your online data profile using the application which will go through all your saved password account and recommend security actions and highlight security concerns such as multiple sites using the same password, easy to guess passwords, week passwords or incorrect information associated with an online account. Data breaches may include such information leaks as email addresses, credit card details and other personal identifiable information.

If a data breach has occurred on a specific internet service that you use, then it is your prerogative and responsibility to see if you still want to do business with this specific internet provider or if there is another similar internet service provider who will better ensure the safety and security of your personal data. If so, and you do want to move to another service provider then do not say to the existing service provider the reason for cancelation or moving service provider if it requires exporting of data to a new platform as this may cause additional barrier or hurdles put in your way to slow down this transition.

It is the case that when a data breach occurs, some companies may choose to delay for substantial periods of time to the public that a data breach has occurred and the scale and scope of the breach.

Companies are legal obliged to report to data controller with twenty-four hours of initial detection that a data breach has occurred. If this is not the case, the company is open to legal repercussions against them. If you feel or know that you are the victim of a data breach, then there are several technical and legal recourses that you can undertake.

Firstly, if a data breach does occur with a service provider that you are using, do not add any new information to you existing user account.

Secondly, record last time you accessed account and the type of information populated in you user account.

Thirdly, were necessary or possible change account and user information and where optional fields exist in account creation, leave them blank as they are not required.

Fourthly, review what your available options are for migrating to a new service provider. If bank accounts details or card details have been compromised, then change as soon as possible.

Fifthly, ensure the same level of security exists with all your internet account as the weakest link will be targeted successful first. Ensuring consistent layers of security across all your internet activity both on devices you own, use and public and private network should always be maintained and believing one form of technology, network connectivity or device is more secure than another is not a good approach to internet security.

Large data breaches only occur with internet usage and most internet users' personal details have most likely compromised at least once in their lifetime. The severity of data breaches can vary from personal details of name and email address being compromised to more complex data breaches including medical records, financial records, election records and a person's complete career records. These matters are dealt seriously by government agencies employed to manage these situations, but we are the purveyor of our own personal information, and we are responsible for whom we choose to give this information to.

As such in some instances, it is impossible to avoid being 'put on the system', however we should never feel that one system is all systems in that we feel that all IT systems share information and once it's out there it is out there. This is not the case as every data collection point needs a reason for collecting personal data, how this person's data is stored, for how long and method of destruction when stored information is no longer required.

These data protection acts in various jurisdictions protect individuals' users' privacy and addresses data concerns, however the weakest link in a data protection chain is the individual. This is where a person employed by an agency with the intention of harvest and leek personal information for person gain. This should be seen for what it is. They are not acting as heroes or in the people's interest but only in their own interest. Leaking information, no matter what the intention does not have the consent of the individual involved and who's data it is in the first place. This is equivalent to finding stolen goods and passing them off as you own.

As we can see information is powerful and valuable and in the wrong hands and is potentially destructive. Governments agencies responsible for tracking down for such interest are only acting in the best interest of the owners of such information and information it is about. Wiki leaks did not contribute to any positive impact. This type of information has been collected for generations and by it leaking this information did not contribute to a new dialogue, public debate, new legislation, or new awareness but instead effect the lives of thousands of non-related persons around the world. They happened to work in an environment where eavesdropping, data collection, spying and tailing individuals is part of their daily life, but this is the life that they signed up for in the first place. Ask anybody who works in the diplomatic Corp, military, police, or security services if this is not the case you will no doubt receive a stoned walled response which says it all.

The outcome of wiki leaks is increased spending for continuous background and present round checks for individuals. Individuals' beliefs can change over time from when they joined an organisation. These vetting or background check usually happened when an individual joined and organisation. This evolved to three years. Now it is generally ongoing and always present. It goes back to the adage if you have nothing to hide then you have nothing to worry about. Continuous background checks are now part of a lot of people live and they of the acceptance that their employer knows all their deepest and darkest secrets. This may sound scary, but it is the price you must pay to work in certain sectors. Privacy legislation is addressed by the complete understanding and cooperation of all parties concerned.

Chapter 14 – Conclusion

So, this book does cover aspects of internet security and how simple things can make a big difference to your security. It was not meant to be a deep dive into everything internet but to make the public aware of the types of security issues that do exist on the internet and how these risks are increasing in numbers and severity.

So, you have been warned. Do don't take your internet profile, personal profile, and internet security for granted and thinks it's the job of the government or police. At the end of the day, you and you alone are responsible for your own personal security, and this includes everything you log onto a device or use and internet related service.

Simple habits will make a big difference, but the best advises is still the same, do not share your personal information with anybody or organisation that you can not verify their identity, existence, or reason for wanting your information in the first place.

When I address the reason for writing this book in the first place, to help those of the pre internet era navigate the murky waters of the internet age, this book will righten their internet ship and ensure safe passage through otherwise dangerous and dark waters.

Thank you for reading, please take on board what you believe will make the internet a safe place for you and those closes to you and safe travels.

Don't miss out!

Visit the website below and you can sign up to receive emails whenever DG publishes a new book. There's no charge and no obligation.

https://books2read.com/r/B-A-TWTGB-MTABD

BOOKS 2 READ

Connecting independent readers to independent writers.

www.ingramcontent.com/pod-product-compliance
Lightning Source LLC
Chambersburg PA
CBHW020345180726
47991CB00021B/2534